OUTLAW TALES
of Oklahoma

OUTLAW TALES
of Oklahoma

True Stories of the Sooner State's Most Infamous
Crooks, Culprits, and Cutthroats

Second Edition

Robert Barr Smith

TWODOT®

GUILFORD, CONNECTICUT
HELENA, MONTANA
AN IMPRINT OF GLOBE PEQUOT PRESS

A · TWODOT® · BOOK

Map by M. A. Dubè © Morris Book Publishing, LLC
Project Editor: Lauren Brancato
Layout Artist: Sue Murray

Library of Congress Cataloging-in-Publication Data is available on file.

ISBN 978-0-7627-7262-9

Printed in the United States of America

10 9 8 7 6 5 4 3 2

Contents

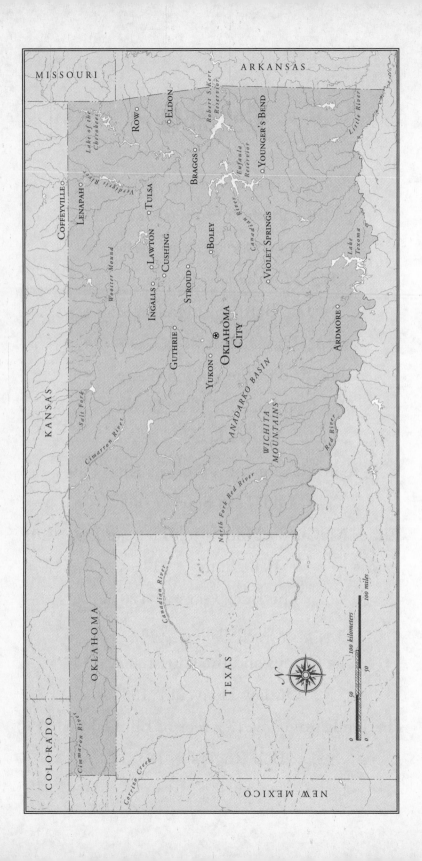

Introduction

In the years after the Civil War, Oklahoma—Indian Territory in those far-off days—was as tough a country as this nation ever saw. The Five Civilized Tribes—Cherokee, Choctaw, Chickasaw, Creek, and Seminole—pushed off their ancestral land in the southeastern United States, settled in this wild country. In the territory they had their own system of law enforcement, judges and courts and police, and the system worked very well. Trouble was, they had no jurisdiction over whites.

Many of the white settlers who flooded Indian Territory were fine stock, just people looking for a new start, for a place to call their own, plant their crops, and raise their children. But there were also the others, the scum of the earth, men who

Judge Parker's long arm: a collection of the most famous and veteran deputy US marshals *Western History Collections, University of Oklahoma Libraries*

thought nothing of killing another man because they wanted his boots or his horse or his land . . . or, as in one case, because the killer wanted fish bait and his victim was handy. The tribes had their own "bad hats" as well, but by and large the majority of the offenders were white.

But violence, all kinds of violence, was epidemic. Some of it was small-time. In March of 1896, the *Indian Journal* matter-of-factly reported that

> [a]t a dance in the Nocus Harjo neighborhood one night last week one Royal Junking let off his Winchester in the midst of a row. The ball wounded two men in the arm, passed through the wall, killed a dog on the outside and entered a tree. The dance then proceeded.

Such happenings were routine stuff in the territory. But there were other much more serious doings. Take this fairly commonplace *Muskogee Phoenix* story of July 1896:

> A serious shooting affray is reported from Oolagah. Eli Rogers shot and instantly killed Nick Rogers and at the same time Sharp Rogers was shot by Sam Rogers. The trouble began at Huse Rogers' house . . . and is the result of an old feud. . . . [T]he killing is the outcome of the fight in which Bub Trainor lost his life more than a year ago. The shot received by Sharp Rogers will prove fatal.

The Indian Territory was infested with outlaws on the run from other places, looking only for somewhere to hide while they continued their depredations. Others of their kind were homegrown. Most of them died young, and most of those expired of terminal lead poisoning. Some perished at the end of a rope. But while they lived, they killed and robbed and raped, and they made the territory a terribly dangerous place for law-abiding people.

Introduction

The only white man's law in Indian Territory was the Federal District Court for the Western District of Arkansas. The court, with only a single judge, sat at Fort Smith, Arkansas, with jurisdiction over much of Arkansas and the wild expanse of Indian Territory. The actions—and the enormous achievements—of that court must be seen in the context of the times, days when law-abiding people had to deal with ruthless human predators. Dealing with hard men required hard measures. The court provided just that.

It was a colossal task, but the times produced a man equal to the job. He was called Isaac Parker, and he has gone down in history as the "hanging judge," largely on the strength of a couple of dubious accounts of the operations of his court. In fact Judge Parker was a devout man, devoted to his family, his work, and God. He was even known to preach from the bench to men sentenced to hang, urging them to make their peace with their creator. He dealt with depraved criminals harshly, but both his conscience and the spirit of the times required it.

His long arm was the marshal service, about two hundred deputy US marshals at any given time, riding west of Fort Smith into the vastness of the lawless country beyond, more than seventy thousand square miles of it. They carried a sheaf of warrants, and they sometimes took a posse with them, but often they rode alone. More than sixty of them died in the line of duty out beyond the Arkansas River.

Judge Parker sentenced some 160 men to the gallows at Fort Smith, and 79 of them actually were hanged: murderers and rapists, white, black, Indian, and mixed blood. Judge Parker played no favorites.

A little at a time, Judge Parker and his deputy marshals brought to the wild lands a semblance of law and order, and the hangings at Fort Smith must be seen in the context of the lawless times. During Judge Parker's years on the bench, the docket of his court listed a prodigious 13,490 felonies, committed by men—and a few women—of the most depraved kind. Judge Parker sat from 1875 until the autumn of 1896. He quite literally wore himself out in the service of the law, and he died in harness. One of Fort Smith's leading attorneys summed him up quite accurately in conversation with a Saint Louis reporter:

> Judge Parker is learned in the law; he is conscientious of
> the administration of it. He has a kind heart and a big
> soul. He is absolutely faithful to his home ties. All I could
> say of him for days would be summed up in this: He is a
> good man.

It was a fitting epitaph for the man who did so much to tame Indian Territory. The chapters that follow vividly illustrate the vermin that he, and other lawmen, battled with on a daily basis. And won.

Bloodbath at Goingsnake

From the inside of the courtroom, juror George Blackwood saw the grim-faced posse heading for the courthouse door. He also saw they were armed to the teeth. The posse was coming inside to get Zeke Proctor. Near the doorway White Sut Beck, a member of the posse with a score to settle, shoved aside an Indian policeman and stormed into the courthouse. Inevitably, somebody fired a shot, and then everything broke loose. White Sut pulled down on Zeke Proctor, but Johnson Proctor, Zeke's brother, grabbed White Sut's weapon and took one barrel full in his own chest. Johnson, mortally hurt, still hung onto the shotgun, forcing the second shot down toward the floor. Zeke was hit in the foot by a couple of buckshot, but his brother had saved his life. Zeke's defense counsel, Mose Alberty, was hit with two shotgun rounds and went down, dying.

As gunfire roared in the log schoolhouse, men on both sides began to fall. Nobody knows how many men Zeke shot, but he produced a weapon from somewhere, probably a revolver, and the range was point-blank. He took shelter in a convenient chimney corner, which gave him at least a little cover.

At the door Sam Beck stepped in front of White Sut, and somebody cut him down. Then White Sut dropped, and more and more men fell in agony as weapons roared inside and outside the courthouse. The Beck faction quickly realized they were badly outgunned. They scattered then, those who could still stand, and the firing and the shouting died away.

As the smoke blew away, the ground was littered with bodies. Four corpses lay in a welter of blood inside the school-house door. Three more lifeless bodies were sprawled outside. A few paces away lay another corpse, and a badly wounded man lay moaning behind the building.

And another was dying in a nearby clump of bushes.

Judge Sixkiller had two buckshot in his wrist, and lawyer Alberty lay dead near Johnson Proctor, both men elderly and unarmed. One juror had a hole in his shoulder, and several others also had wounds, most of them minor. Close by, in Mrs. Whitmire's house, Deputy Marshal Owen was dying, gasping that he had tried his best to hold back the Becks.

Zeke Proctor was being held and charged for the murder of one of Sam Beck's kin. Proctor never meant to kill Polly Beck, but he was after blood. He wanted to put a bullet into Jim Kesterson, the white man with whom Polly lived at Hilderbrand's Mill. When Zeke confronted Kesterson, both men reached for their guns, and Zeke was a lot faster. Trouble was, as he squeezed off a round, Polly threw her body in front of Kesterson to shield him, and the bullet meant for Kesterson killed her. Then Kesterson fled for his life.

What happened to Zeke Proctor can only be understood against that background and the bloody canvas of the Civil War. Like most of the tribes, the Cherokees were split between North and South. A majority supported the Confederacy, but some adhered to the North. Zeke chose the North, enlisting in July of 1862 and serving three years in an outfit called the Indian Home Guard. It is known that he was wounded at least once in fighting. Old friendships between Cherokees serving the Union as Zeke did, and others of his tribe wearing the Confederate uniform, crumbled, and the seeds of postwar trouble were sowed.

Zeke was a farmer, like most of his people, and served as a lawman in his district. Zeke's parents christened him Ezekial, an appropriate biblical name. He came of ancient English stock, son of a family that had first seen the shores of America in the early 1600s, but he was also a half-blood Cherokee. At least in his youth, Zeke had a distinct fondness for strong spirits and loud roistering, and for shooting up saloons.

By 1890 he owned three farms, ten structures of various kinds, a large stock of produce, and a sizable collection of domestic animals. In addition to his thriving farms, he may have maintained more than one wife, but in those days polygamy was neither uncommon nor unlawful in the Cherokee Nation.

A prosperous and respected citizen, he would not have ended up on the wrong end of the law had it not been for the deep family pride all Cherokees knew, the bitter dregs of Civil War divisiveness and anger, and the deep-seated chasm between the Keetoowahs and others in the Cherokee Nation.

Although Zeke hadn't intended to hurt Polly, once the Cherokee justice system took jurisdiction of his case, the fat was in the fire. There were problems from the start. If the Becks were numerous and influential, so were the Proctors. The two families had taken leading parts in Cherokee government. They had been close once, too, but the Civil War had changed some of that friendship.

The clash between the Proctors and Becks, between the traditionalist Keetoowahs and white man's law, was further aggravated by a jurisdictional dispute between Indian and US courts. Zeke himself was unquestionably Cherokee, and Kesterson was

Cherokee by adoption. Because that was so, the US–Cherokee treaty seemed specifically to solve the question of who had the right to jurisdiction. "[T]he judicial tribunals of the [Cherokee] nation shall be allowed to retain exclusive jurisdiction in all civil and criminal cases, arising within their country, in which members of the nation, by nativity or adoption, shall be the only parties, or where the cause of action shall arise in the Cherokee Nation except as otherwise provided in this treaty."

It was hard to find a judge or a prosecutor who wasn't somehow related to the Proctors. The regular judge was disqualified because he was related to the Proctors—to both sides, for that matter. So also was a second. At last Chief Downing appointed Blackhaw Sixkiller as judge, and Sixkiller quickly set about getting the case to trial.

Everybody was expecting trouble, so the case was scheduled to be heard on April 15, in the Whitmire schoolhouse, rather than the Goingsnake district courthouse. The school building, near what is now Christie, Oklahoma, was farther away from Beck country than the courthouse. Besides, the school was a solid log building, and it had only one door and fewer windows than the courthouse. It would therefore be easier to defend in case of trouble.

Because the Proctor family was large and well connected, and Zeke was a prominent Keetoowah, the Beck family was not sure their idea of justice would be done. And so, on April 11, Jim Kesterson and a party of Becks rode into Fort Smith to hedge their bets. The US magistrate issued a warrant for Zeke's arrest, apparently on the fanciful notion that, in spite of the clear language of the treaty, the United States had jurisdiction over offenses against white people. And Kesterson was white, adopted Cherokee or not. The magistrate also issued warrants for seven other men, including Judge Sixkiller—and added a bizarre touch by issuing warrants for the entire jury.

He also issued some very peculiar instructions to the two unfortunate deputy marshals sent to serve the warrants. They were to wait until the results of the Cherokee trial were known, and if Zeke was convicted, they were to return to Fort Smith without taking any action. In case of an acquittal, however, their mission was to arrest Zeke and the others named in the warrants and return them to Fort Smith.

On the day of trial, the makeshift courthouse was jammed with people, many of them Proctor partisans armed to the teeth. Outside stood a dense crowd of Cherokees, eager to hear the proceedings . . . or to be handy in case of trouble. Among them were a number of Beck partisans, also armed, wearing twigs of wild plum blossom in their hats as badges of support.

Inside, the court clerk sat near Judge Sixkiller. Zeke's lawyer, Mose Alberty, sat on the judge's right. Zeke sat next to Alberty. Tom Walkingstick, one of his guards, stood close to Zeke.

At about eleven in the morning, a posse appeared—mostly Beck partisans—led by Deputy US Marshals J. G. Peavy and J. G. Owens, both well respected and well liked in the Indian Nations. Owens ordered his posse men to stay out of the courthouse until the verdict was reached, but Owens quickly lost control.

The posse men dismounted, formed a rough column of twos, and pushed through the crowd toward the door. Other armed Beck partisans in the crowd outside joined them. Nobody doubted they meant business, because they were cocking their weapons as they came. In the lead was Surry White

Sut Beck, cradling his double-barreled shotgun. Once the posse men were inside the schoolhouse, the bloodbath began.

The Becks took terrible casualties. Black Sut, Samuel, and William Beck were dead or dying. So were William Hicks, Jim Ward, George Selvidge, and Riley Woods. White Sut Beck was seriously hurt, although he would survive, and Isaac Vann had a bad elbow wound.

In addition to Johnson Proctor, the Proctors lost Andrew Palone, a Civil War veteran of the Pea Ridge fight. Several others, both partisans and bystanders, had suffered more or less minor wounds. Zeke's only wound was the buckshot from White Sut's weapon; he could still fight and ride.

After the bloodbath Widow Whitmire got her teenage boys to hitch the family mules to a wagon and begin to collect the dead, dying, and wounded. The bodies of those killed were conveniently arranged on the Whitmire front porch so their kinfolk could collect them easily. The wounded were gently carried inside, to be cared for by Mrs. Whitmire and others.

On the next day the jury reconvened at Capt. Arch Scraper's house nearby to finish the job. Zeke was there too, announcing that he would not give up his right to be present at his own trial. Wounds and all, the jury deliberated long enough to acquit Zeke and then intelligently departed in some haste, on the sound theory that Fort Smith would send more marshals, or more Becks would appear, or both.

James Huckleberry, the US marshal, furious over the carnage, sent a twenty-one-man posse down to Goingsnake, but by the time the lawmen arrived two days later, nearly everybody had scattered. The deputy marshal in command, Charles F. Robinson, wisely decided not to launch a fruitless pursuit into the hills and thickets of the district. Robinson had brought along two doctors, Julian Fields and C. F. Pierce, who set to work to do what they could for the wounded.

Though wounded, Zeke was nowhere to be found. Escorted by a group of nearly fifty heavily armed Keetoowahs, he was headed for the toughest and most inaccessible parts of the Cherokee lands. Judge Sixkiller was also gone to the tall timber, as were most of the jurors.

In spite of Robinson's intelligent decision not to pursue Zeke, it took time for all the bad blood to die away. For a while afterward great tension existed between the Cherokees and anybody who was or looked like a deputy marshal. There was some gunplay and some deaths, and even Proctor family members attributed some of the killings to Zeke. One thing was clear: No marshal, no matter how efficient or courageous, was going to catch Zeke.

Inevitably, Zeke was indicted for murder in the death of Deputy Marshal Owens, charged with some twenty others, including those of the judge and members of the jury. In the flowery, verbose, tedious legal language of the age, Zeke, with "a certain pistol then and there loaded and charged with gunpowder and twenty leaden bullets . . . then and there feloniously and willfully and of his malice aforethought did shoot and discharge; and that . . . with the leaden bullets aforesaid out of the pistol aforesaid then and there by force of the gunpowder shot and sent forth as aforesaid Jacob Owens in and upon the left side of him . . . " and on and on, ad nauseam, including allegations of aiding and abetting murder against a whole host of other Cherokees. The curious reference to a weapon loaded with twenty rounds remains obscure.

In any case Zeke would not be tried again. Hiding out in the hills of Cherokee country, escorted and protected by Keetoowah partisans and kinfolk, he would remain free until at last some of the old bad blood died away.

And so peace of a kind returned to Goingsnake District. But it did not include Zeke Proctor and White Sut Beck. For many years each man watched his back trail, kept his weapons close, wondered what lay hidden in the woods up ahead. Each man was carefully watched over by his kinfolk.

As a testament to the support he held at home, Zeke became Cherokee senator from Goingsnake District in 1877 and was elected sheriff in 1894. In the autumn of 1891, Zeke was appointed a deputy US marshal. He rode for tough, indefatigable federal judge Isaac Parker, all the law there was west of Fort Smith. Marshaling must have agreed with Zeke, who knew every trail and hideout in the Nations. He renewed his contract in February of 1895.

Zeke Proctor died at home at seventy-seven, in February of 1907, not of hot lead or cold steel, but of pneumonia. He's buried in the Proctor family plot in Johnson cemetery, five miles west of Siloam Springs. His monument is the tallest in the cemetery, and that is as it should be. Respectable in his old age, Zeke had never entirely forsaken the old ways. His last words, his granddaughter said, were, "Feed the boys good." He meant the outlaw Wickliffe brothers, then lying low in Zeke's barn.

But before Zeke died, and long years after the rains had washed away the clotted blood outside the Whitmire schoolhouse, White Sut Beck and Zeke Proctor finally met in the land office at Tahlequah, and after all the years stood face-to-face at last, two old and mortal enemies.

Finally, White Sut Beck spoke. "Proctor," he said, "we're too old to fight. But I'm game and I know you are too. I'll walk away if you will."

And then, without saying more, the two tough, proud old men turned and left the land office by different ways. The feud was over, without formality, without fanfare, without speeches. Nobody had backed down. Nobody had won; nobody had lost.

Which was how the long feud should have ended.

The Cook Gang
The Trash of the Territory

Cherokee policeman Sequoyah Houston went down dying, and the rest of his posse returned fire, riddling Effie Crittenden's house, shooting at Cherokee Bill Goldsby and the Cook boys, Bill and Jim.

As Indians, Cherokee Bill and the two Cooks were entitled to tribal land claim payments by the federal government, to be picked up at the Cherokee capital of Tahlequah. But because they were wanted by the law, they had anticipated some difficulty collecting the payments in person. They gave written permission to Effie Crittenden to collect their shares.

The Cherokee posse got wind of this and rode off to Effie's home, hoping to collect the outlaws. In the gunfight that followed, Effie prudently crawled behind the cookstove while the bullets flew. Houston, a respected full-blood member of the Cherokee police, was shot down in the gunfight. This group of Cherokee police, often called the Lighthorse, vowed revenge.

The Cooks' sister, Lou, saddled their horses for the men as they fought off the law, helping them escape. They got away all right, but not unscathed. Jim Cook took eight buckshot pellets in his body. The story goes that Effie, asked if Goldsby was part of the outlaw gang, said, "No. It was Cherokee Bill." It's a nice story, but in all probability Goldsby had carried his famous handle long before he may have been referred to by that name on this bloody day.

Bill Cook, leader of the gang that carried his name *Western History Collections, University of Oklahoma Libraries*

Now the pursuit was joined by an angry group of Houston's relatives and friends, while the local doctor who patched up Jim Cook did his work at gunpoint. The other outlaws threatened the doctor with death if he told anybody that they had visited him, but the three were soon seen crossing the Arkansas on a ferry.

A gunfight between Cherokee Bill and Deputy US Marshal John McGill soon followed. Neither man was hurt, and the two unwounded outlaws fled when McGill was reinforced. Jim Cook couldn't run, however, and was captured, as the *Muskogee Indian Journal* put it, "shot as nearly to pieces as it is possible to be and live." He was held to be tried for murder by the Cherokee tribal court at Tahlequah.

Like most western outlaw bands, the Cook Gang was a collection of losers, banded together to steal what honest people earned, quite willing to kill any poor soul who got in their way. For sheer meanness their only close rivals were the vicious Buck Gang (more about them later).

Cherokee Bill (3), on his way to face "Hanging Judge" Isaac Parker at Fort Smith, Arkansas *Western History Collections, University of Oklahoma Libraries*

The Cooks never partook of the sort of lasting notoriety showered on other equally contemptible but more colorful gangs. The James-Younger and Dalton Gangs stole the spotlight, but nobody cared much about the Cooks. Like most of the outlaws of the time, most of them ended up dead early in life.

The Cooks were named after their leader, William Tuttle Cook, inevitably called Bill. The gang's heyday was the mid-1890s, and for a time they were such a pestilence that men— and women—feared to travel the roads and paths of the eastern territory, even in broad daylight.

The Cooks bore not the slightest resemblance to Robin Hood: They robbed anybody of anything and made no distinction between rich and poor, Indian and white.

Bill Cook was one-eighth Cherokee, growing up over on the Neosho River north of Fort Gibson. His first brush with the law was on a charge of selling whiskey, a federal offense in Indian Territory. He could have stopped there, but he didn't. For a while he punched cattle and even worked as a posse man for a federal deputy marshal, Will Smith. But in 1894 his kid brother Jim was charged with larceny and then compounded the problem by jumping bail. Bill joined him, a demonstration of his proclivity for the wrong side of the law. The two soon joined forces with a longtime acquaintance, Crawford Goldsby.

Goldsby was a handsome young man of mixed blood, in various proportions Cherokee, Sioux, white, black, and Mexican. Deserted by his father, ignored by a stepfather, cordially disliked by his elder sister's husband, Mose Brown, he grew up wild. He rejoiced in an exotic handle acquired someplace early in life. He was called Cherokee Bill.

In 1892 he was hanging around the town of Catoosa, working in a livery stable and at whatever else came his way. He could not have been content with this workaday, law-abiding existence. In those days Catoosa was a wild and woolly settlement, a railhead town that received the trail herds out of Texas. With the cattle came the cowboys, young, full of beans, hungry for whiskey and the pleasures of the bedroom, ready for a fight or a frolic. Trouble was easy to find on Catoosa's streets and in its saloons—it was Cherokee Bill's kind of town.

In Catoosa, Bill met a couple of charter members of the gang. Thurman "Skeeter" Baldwin was a cowboy in his mid-twenties. Sam McWilliams was a seventeen-year-old wannabe rustler who answered to "the Verdigris Kid" or "Mosquita."

Toward the end of 1893, Cherokee Bill attended a dance in Fort Gibson and quarreled over a girl with whom he was enamored, no doubt fueled by whiskey. The end of it was a fistfight in which Cherokee Bill was decisively pummeled by a freedman, Jake Lewis. Next day a vengeful Cherokee Bill renewed the fight. But this time there were no fists; he simply ambushed his rival in a stable and drove two pistol bullets into Lewis.

Lewis survived, but Cherokee Bill did not wait around to discuss the rights and wrongs of the incident. Instead, he prudently fled and joined up with Bill Cook and his brother Jim, Skeeter Baldwin, and other equally worthless hoodlums. The gang went off stealing horses and dodging the law, because Cherokee Bill knew nearly every pig trail of the Indian Territory. Friends urged Cherokee Bill to surrender, a logical and prudent notion—both he and Lewis were Cherokee freedmen, so the Cherokee court had jurisdiction and the sentence would probably be relatively light. Cherokee Bill elected to stay on the run.

And then in the spring of 1894 came the payment of the "Cherokee Strip Money," almost $7 million of compensation for lost territory to be paid to members of the Cherokee Nation at Tahlequah. Besides the payees and legitimate business-men, Tahlequah swarmed with snake oil salesmen, gamblers, whiskey sellers, thieves, a man who ran a steam-driven merry-go-round, and an assortment of feather merchants offering all manner of things on credit.

Violence inevitably followed. Among the more serious offenses were a stage holdup and the murder of a woman by one Levi Sanders, promptly shot dead by his victim's son. The murder of Houston by the Cooks angered the Cherokee Nation, whose police would never forget. Now Cook and Cherokee Bill were wanted men, and if they had had any sense at all, they would have left Indian Territory altogether. But instead of fleeing they made outlawry a full-time business. With the Verdigris Kid and Skeeter Baldwin, they set out to make a career of oppressing the righteous. To these they added other outlaws and would-be felons: Lon Gordon; Jess Snyder (aka "Buck"); Elmer Lucas (aka "Chicken"); Curt Dayson; Jim French; a killer called Buss Luckey; George Sanders; and Henry Munson, a penitentiary alumnus who dubbed himself "Texas Jack Starr."

George Sanders, brother of the late unlamented murderer Levi, was a particularly vicious sort. He'd once robbed a man by holding a revolver to his victim's baby's head, threatening to kill it if the man did not give up his money. French had already tried to kill a couple of people and was also wanted for mail robbery.

This collection was commonly referred to as the "Cook Gang," although its members committed their crimes in pairs and small bunches about as often as they defied the law en masse. In July of 1894, for example, Cherokee Bill and Jim French held up the general store in little Wetumka; in the same month Cherokee Bill and Munson robbed Dick Richards, railroad station agent at Nowata. True to his salt, Richards went for his pistol, and Cherokee Bill shot him in the neck and killed him.

Less than a day later, six outlaws stopped the Muskogee–Fort Gibson stage and robbed the passengers. The holdup men wore masks, but the press concluded—probably correctly—that the evildoers were the Cook Gang. About an hour later the same bunch robbed a well-known Cherokee man.

Still in July, the depot at Illinois was robbed once, the Fort Gibson depot twice, and a man from the hamlet of Muldrow murdered and robbed of about $1,000. At midmonth the gang held up a Frisco train at a tiny place called Red Fork. This time the haul was meager: a few dollars, a box of cigars, and a jug of whiskey. None of the gang inspected the express agent's receipt book, into which he had stuffed a large amount of cash.

So far the gang's holdups had been easy, no doubt inflating their own opinions of themselves. But now all of that was about to change. At the end of July, they barged into the Lincoln County Bank in Chandler only to find that the time lock on the bank's safe was still set. When a sick bank employee, ordered to open the safe, fainted from his illness, one of the frustrated outlaws took a shot at the man as he lay on the floor.

Their next mistake was both callous and stupid—they killed the popular town barber, shooting him down simply because he shouted that the bank was being robbed. The shot, far more likely than a yell to alert the town, brought on Sheriff Claude Parker. Parker stood boldly in the middle of the street and emptied his pistol at the outlaws, hitting one horse and one man.

Parker then raised a small posse and pursued. More shooting followed, and four miles out of town, the posse collected Chicken Lucas, shot in both legs and probably displeased that the gang had galloped off and left him, taking his horse with them.

While he was in the Guthrie lockup, Lucas kept talking. The other robbers, he said, had been Bill Cook, Cherokee Bill, Gordon, and Munson, and he helpfully volunteered the information that he had ridden along on the Red Fork train robbery.

The gang surfaced again on August 2, and on that day a tough band of Euchee Indians jumped them at the home of Munson's uncle. In the battle that followed, Munson was killed and Curt Dayson captured. Lon Gordon took a round through the lungs and died shortly afterward in Sapulpa. Cook, Snyder, Baldwin, and Cherokee Bill got away.

In early September Jim French and one Meigs decided to hold up Robert Bean at his home near Tahlequah. They called Bean from his house, and he obliged them by coming out, but the trouble was he came out smokin', guns firing. He shot Meigs in the chest and the outlaws fled empty-handed.

Then, on the night of September 14, Cook, Snyder, Baldwin, and Cherokee Bill rode into Okmulgee. Much of the town being absent at a baseball game, they had little trouble robbing some $600 from the local store. Next they attacked the depot at Fort Gibson, got another $300, and galloped out of town spraying bullets. The next day they robbed a lone traveler and then split up. Cook and two other outlaws then robbed a group of coal miners of whatever pittance they may have had.

They missed a real haul in Claremore when the station agent, warned that suspicious-looking riders were coming to town, prudently evacuated his funds on the outbound train. The gang again left empty-handed. Twenty miles away at Chouteau they got a sack of silver and gold and silver certificates from the American Express agent. They also robbed a railroad employee of a measly $35.

By now the honest people of eastern Indian Territory had had a great bellyful of the Cooks. One politician told the *Kansas City Times* that "people are afraid to travel," which was understandable in view of the gang's propensity for robbing anybody and anything. One cable to the Indian Affairs administration in Washington pleaded that "[a]ffairs here are in a desperate condition; business is suspended, the people generally intimidated and private individuals robbed every day and night."

A Muskogee resident remembered a friend placing a six-gun on the table and commenting, "I understand the Cook Gang is coming in tonight." Muskogee merchants organized a home guard and installed an alarm system to alert the defenders. According to the *Fort Smith Indian Journal*, US Marshal George Crump offered $250 a head reward for Cook Gang members, dead or alive. His offer named, besides Cook and Cherokee Bill, an astonishing number of wanted men, including Bill Doolin, the Slaughter Kid—a sobriquet of Bitter Creek Newcomb—and a host of lesser lights.

Now the lawlessness got even worse. On October 20 the gang wrecked a Katy (Missouri-Kansas-Texas Railroad) train at a town called Coretta, throwing a switch and sending the train smashing into a line of boxcars on the siding. Firing their weapons, presumably to cow the passengers, the gang robbed the express car of about $500 and then went through the train, robbing individual passengers.

By this time the gang's depredations were hurting the economy of eastern Indian Territory. Travelers left their valuables at home whenever they could. Banks charged a premium for issuing negotiable drafts. Pacific Express suspended its money order business. Many businesses closed at nightfall, and businessmen who had to move money concealed it in various ingenious ways. The *State Capital* reported that "[o]ne traveling man brought $3,000 out sealed in a horse collar; another drummer brought out $1,500 in the bottom of a sack of oats."

Things were so bad that the Indian agent at Muskogee wired Washington, asking for military help to break what he called "the state of siege." The gang's crimes were prime fodder for the many people who wanted all of Oklahoma made a state. Newspapers both in and out of the territory clamored for statehood as the sovereign remedy for this crime wave. "How much longer," grumbled the *Afton Weekly Herald*, "is Bill Cook going to be allowed to terrorize the Indian Territory?"

Still not smart enough—or maybe too arrogant—to leave the territory, the gang split up again and went right on with their crimes. Cook, Baldwin, Snyder, and one William Farris robbed a trading post on November 2 and two days later held up an emigrant family on the road.

The Verdigris Kid and Cherokee Bill rode into the town of Lenapah and went into the Shufeldt store, where they forced Shufeldt to open the safe. They cleaned out the safe and robbed the owner as well, stole some merchandise and ammunition, and held up the post office for good measure. And here tragedy struck. When a harmless man working next door looked into

Shufeldt's from a window, Cherokee Bill wantonly killed him with a single rifle round.

The outlaws made a clean getaway, but the deputy marshals used an informer to locate the pair. A posse led by the formidable Heck Bruner and Heck Thomas found them at a house up on the Caney River. In the inevitable firefight that followed, somebody got a bullet into Cherokee Bill's leg and another bullet killed the Verdigris Kid's horse. A deputy marshal, Jim Carson, was shot in the foot, but Cherokee Bill and the Verdigris Kid managed to get away.

The remorseless pursuit by Lighthorse riders and deputy marshals had at last driven Cook and four other outlaws across the Red River into Texas, where they intended to pass their time usefully, robbing trains. A suspicious rancher spotted them, however, and thoughtfully wired Company A of the Texas Rangers at Amarillo. Sgt. W. J. L. Sullivan—called "John L."—collected five other rangers and responded. They silently collared a mounted outlaw sentry and surrounded the building where the gang was hiding.

There was an exchange of gunfire, but then the reports from the house fell away into silence. The rangers broke down the door to find the bandits had fled to the attic. The lawmen heard one of them call out that he wanted to surrender, but somebody else threatened to kill him if he did. Sergeant Sullivan settled the question when he threatened to burn down the house and the gang with it. Cook had gotten away, but the other four hoodlums surrendered.

The prisoners, having been returned to Fort Smith, turned out to be Baldwin, Snyder, Farris, and a local recruit, Charles Turner. Skeeter got thirty years and Farris and Snyder both got

twenty, which prompted Skeeter to comment with some bitterness, "What a hell of a court for a man to plead guilty in."
Turner was acquitted.

Meanwhile, Cherokee Bill had gone to see his stepsister,
Maude Brown, at Talala, and while he was there, he got cross-
ways with her husband, Mose, with whom he had always had
difficulty. When Mose threatened to talk to the law about Cherokee Bill, or Cherokee Bill thought he was going to, the outlaw put
seven Winchester bullets into Mose, whereof he died. Cherokee
Bill celebrated his latest murder by robbing the Kansas–Arkansas
Valley depot at Nowata.

Bill Cook still had the remorseless Sergeant Sullivan on his
back trail. Cook got as far as Roswell, New Mexico, but on
January 11, 1895, the law at last ran him down and took him
without a fight. Returned to Fort Smith, he was invited by tough
judge Isaac Parker to spend the next forty-five years in prison.

While Cook was hearing where he'd soon be living, Jim
French and the Verdigris Kid, on March 28, stuck up a store in
Fort Gibson, helping themselves not only to the available cash,
but to new suits and a variety of other clothing.

Meanwhile, Cherokee Bill, deeply enamored of a young lady
named Maggie Glass, agreed to a rendezvous at the home of
her older cousin, one-time deputy marshal Ike Rogers. Rogers
had been discharged from the marshal service for conniving
with outlaws, and he earnestly wished reinstatement. Marshal
Crump promised Rogers that he would consider reinstatement
if Rogers would help bring in Cherokee Bill.

So in early February of 1895, Rogers enlisted a neighbor,
Clint Scales, to help him lay Cherokee Bill by the heels and
invited both Maggie and her suitor to visit him. As always,

Cherokee Bill was alert and wary; he did not trust Rogers at all. Neither did Maggie, who urged the outlaw to leave.

So Cherokee Bill stayed on at Rogers's place and held his Winchester constantly on his knees. He refused a drink of whiskey—which Rogers had thoughtfully spiked with morphine—and the men played cards most of the night. When they finally turned in at about 4:00 a.m., Rogers shared a bed with Cherokee Bill, but each time Rogers moved, he did also.

It was not until after breakfast that Rogers got his chance. When Cherokee Bill rolled a cigarette and reached down to the fireplace for a coal to light it with, Rogers bashed him in the head with a chunk of wood. A wild wrestling match followed, until Rogers and Scales finally subdued Cherokee Bill.

He was taken to Fort Smith and was tried in February 1895, and on April 13 Judge Parker sentenced him to hang for murder. He was hanged on March 17, 1896. He had no last words, in spite of the oft-repeated fable that when asked whether he wanted to say something, he answered, "I came here to die, not to make a speech."

When Cherokee Bill was jailed, the next bandit to fall was Jim French, on a bitter cold day in February 1895. He went to Catoosa with a new partner, Jess Cochran, who called himself Kid Swanson, and Bitter Creek Newcomb. They decided to rob the Reynolds general store, and the neophyte Cochran botched the job by firing through the office door to gain admission, then charging through to collect the money.

What Cochran collected was a shotgun charge fired by clerk Tommy Watkins, who had been seated inside the office. French fired through the window, mortally wounding the store manager, Sam Irwin, who was lying on a cot in the office.

Watkins missed French with his second barrel, leaving him at the bandit's mercy. Enraged at the shooting of Cochran, French was preparing to kill Watkins when the dying Irwin pulled a pistol from beneath his pillow and fired. He drilled French twice in the neck, and the outlaw staggered away from the building, all the fight gone out of him.

Leaving his guns behind, French managed to mount and ride to an old cabin about a mile away. As he hobbled through the front door, the residents vamoosed out the back and a posse appeared, led by the formidable Watkins and his shotgun. After a few exchanges of gunfire, French was gone for good, to the intense relief of the populace. Deputy Marshal Heck Thomas and a couple of citizens delivered what was left of him to Fort Smith where his remains were placed on show according to the custom of the time. Learning of French's death from his cell, Bill Cook made a prophetic comment: "He's better off than we are."

The rest of the gang's brief history is a largely sordid anticlimax. In the spring of 1897, Cherokee Bill's brother, Clarence, murdered Ike Rogers, captor of his brother. Clarence got away and died much later in St. Louis of tuberculosis. Jim Cook escaped from the Cherokee prison in December of 1896, recruited a couple of second-rate helpers, and staged a largely unproductive crime wave. Jim died with his boots on in 1900, shot down in an argument over the ownership of a steer. His brother, Bill, who had started the whole nefarious mess, died in prison in 1900.

Now all that remained of the gang were the bloody memories.

Big-Mouthed Al Jennings
Gross Incompetence

Clouds of powder smoke filled the Cabinet Saloon as Temple Houston stood calmly, firing one careful shot after another. When the shooting stopped, Ed Jennings lay dead on the saloon floor and his brother John was running for his life, hit in the arm and body. The imperturbable Houston was untouched.

The Jennings's brother Al, a lawyer, took umbrage at the death of one brother and the wounding of another and swore bloody vengeance against Houston.

Like Elmer McCurdy, whose story we'll get to later, Al Jennings was a considerable embarrassment to the outlaw profession. And like Elmer he embarked on another career and was infinitely more successful than he had been as a bandit. The difference was that, unlike Elmer, Al didn't have to get himself killed to change careers.

Al was a braggart, but then a lot of criminals are. What really characterized him as an incompetent failure was his persistent blundering. Al was inept to an extent unusual even in a line of work in which intelligence was not a common virtue.

By 1892 his family had moved west from Virginia and settled at the town of El Reno in Canadian County, Oklahoma Territory. His father became a judge in the local court, and Al practiced law in the area with his brothers, John and Ed. Territory lawyers tended to be a tough, aggressive bunch, and the Jennings boys fit right in. It was their misfortune, however, to

Inept Al Jennings, still trying to look tough *Western History Collections, University of Oklahoma Libraries*

meet Temple Houston, an even tougher lawyer. Houston was the son of Sam Houston, "The Father of Texas," and he had been both a district attorney and a state senator down in Brazoria County, a wild panhandle judicial district. Houston was the epitome of the successful frontier lawyer, the Prince Albert coat, ornate vest, and, of course, the Colt revolver. Then he moved north to Woodward in Oklahoma Territory, and it was there that he locked horns with the Jennings boys.

During a hard-fought case, Temple Houston referred to brother Ed as grossly ignorant of the law, which he may well have been. Ed called Houston a liar and started for him. Both men reached for their guns, but others prevented any bloodletting there and then. But after court adjourned, Ed and John adjourned to the Cabinet Saloon where they ran into Houston and ex-lawman Jack Love.

Al later claimed that Ed was "ambushed." However, several newspapers reported that the fight was no more than a common brawl in which the Jennings brothers placed second.

> [T]he quarrel was renewed. Very few words passed
> before all drew their pistols, including [Houston's friend]
> Love. . . . All engaged in a running and dodging fight
> except Houston. The huge man stood up straight and
> emptied his revolver without twitching a muscle. . . .
> Neither Love nor Houston were wounded although
> several bullets passed through their clothes and hats.

Al said dramatically that he was summoned to the saloon, where he knelt beside his brother's corpse and swore to kill the man who had murdered his own flesh and blood.

Love and Houston were duly tried and acquitted after eyewitnesses said Ed Jennings went for his gun first. Al pondered killing Houston but continued to do nothing about it. Instead he wired another brother, Frank, in Denver, and the two ventured into outlawry.

They collected some helpers, Morris and Pat O'Malley, and somewhere along the way were joined by perennial badman Little Dick West, alumnus of the Doolin Gang. They also recruited Dan Clifton, better known by his outlaw handle of "Dynamite Dick," a one-time Dalton and Doolin follower.

Early in June 1897, the new gang held up a store in Violet Springs, one of the infamous Pottawatomie County saloon towns. They then went on to stick up another country store, robbed a party of freighters on the road, and capped their spree by robbing another saloon and all the patrons. Carrying a sackful of money and some stolen whiskey, the little band headed for the woods to relax and enjoy both their whiskey and their success.

Al and Dynamite Dick held up a post office near Claremore. That brought federal officers looking for them. In his autobiography, *Beating Back*, Al said this early raid was only to test out something called a "set-screw," a contraption, he said, that was designed to pop loose locks from safes. This robbery netted the gang $700, which Al said was stolen "just to pay expenses."

But now the law was looking for them, in the person of Deputy US Marshals Paden Tolbert and Bud Ledbetter, who were not good men to have on your back trail. Both were experienced, smart, and tough as nails.

Al became more ambitious. One night he and his cohorts stopped a Santa Fe train near Edmond, just north of Oklahoma City. Three members of the gang boarded the train at Ponca City, well to the north, and transferred to the tender when the train stopped for water at Edmond. The outlaws forced the crew to halt the train a little way down the road, and four more men came out of the darkness to join the first three. The men began shooting and yelling, presumably to keep the train crew and passengers from interfering with the gang's onslaught against the express car. Bullets through the wall of the car forced the agents to open the door, and the gang entered to claim their bonanza.

But then things went sour fast. With the set-screw apparently having been left behind or proven to be unsatisfactory, the gang tried dynamite. Not once but twice they blasted the Wells, Fargo safe, but it refused to open. Defeated, the outlaws ordered the train crew to drive on, and then the outlaws disappeared. Once word of the raid made it to the marshals, posses hit the road from both Guthrie and Kingfisher. However, the posses came up empty-handed.

Having failed at their first try at a train, the gang decided to try it again a couple of weeks later at a spot near Bond Switch, not far from Muskogee. This time the gang stacked railroad ties on the tracks as a roadblock. The train arrived as scheduled but the engineer, instead of jamming on the brakes, used the throttle instead, smashed through the barricade of ties, and disappeared into the night, unrobbed.

With the law on their trail, the gang decided to replenish their money supply by robbing the Santa Fe train depot at Purcell. This time they didn't even get started, because a night watchman saw them skulking near the station. He promptly alerted the station agent, who called the city marshal, who showed up with a posse. Foiled again.

Shortly afterward the law learned that the gang intended to rob the bank in Minco, and the outlaws again were thwarted because a band of citizens mounted a twenty-four-hour guard on the bank. The gang was getting hungry.

So for the next raid the gang chose the Rock Island, selecting a southbound train they thought was carrying some $90,000 in coin headed for banks in Fort Worth. Al decided to rob the train in broad daylight, on the theory that the usual guards were only on duty at night. On the morning of October 1, the gang—six men— forced a railroad section crew to stop the train. The gang hid themselves behind bandannas, except for Al, who had made himself a mask out of a bearskin saddle-pocket and cut eyeholes for visibility.

This time Al had brought lots of dynamite, resolved that he was not to be stopped again by a strong safe. They laid their charge, lit the fuse, and waited for the money. The explosives went off with a colossal roar, tearing the express car to pieces . . . but the safe remained intact. Along the way Al's grotesque mask slipped. Frustrated, the bandits laid another and even heavier charge, and the whole train shook . . . but the safe didn't.

The gang was reduced to tearing open the registered mail and robbing the train crew and the passengers—more than a hundred of them—of their cash and watches. Along the way one of the outlaws shot off a piece of ear of a passenger who was slow to cooperate. This passenger was the only casualty.

This unusual daylight robbery brought several posses converging on the probable escape route of the outlaws. The American Express Company and the Rock Island offered rewards, a total of $800 a head, a good deal of money in those days. But again the gang got away and rendezvoused at a farm near El Reno. There they rested and split up their meager loot. Riding through the cold weather of late October, they moved east toward the town of Cushing.

There they invaded the home of merchant Lee Nutter, waking him, shoving a pistol in his face, and demanding that he go to his store at the front of the building and give them his money. But there wasn't any, because Nutter had sent his store's receipts on to the bank in Guthrie. So the gang had to make do with a couple of weapons and a measly $15, plus a selection of coats and such from the store's stocks, a jug of whiskey, and a bunch of bananas.

Somewhere around Tulsa, Dynamite Dick and Little Dick West left the gang, presumably disgusted with all that work and danger and hardship for practically no reward. Dynamite Dick headed in the direction of Checotah, while West split and rode the other way. Early one morning Dynamite Dick rode past two deputy marshals—Hess Bussey and George Lawson—waiting in ambush. They offered him a chance to surrender, but he was wanted for more than the gang's amateurish crimes. There was a warrant for him for a murder committed back in his days with the Doolin Gang. And so the outlaw whipped up his Winchester and fired. A return shot broke Dynamite Dick's arm and knocked him from the saddle, but he regained his feet and staggered into the brush, leaving his rifle behind him.

The marshals followed, trailing the spatters of Dynamite Dick's blood, and as night fell, they came on a cabin in the woods. They fired warning shots and announced they intended to burn the cabin to the ground. At this an Indian woman and a boy came out. The officers twice commanded them to set fire to the cabin, and on the second command Dynamite Dick ran from the door, shooting as he came. The officers quickly put several holes in him, and he was dead within minutes.

On November 29 the rest of the gang was holed up in a ranch house owned by a Mrs. Harless. After they had eaten supper, they were visited by a neighbor sent by the law to confirm the presence of the bandits. None of them saw the federal posse surrounding the house in the darkness. Deputy Marshals Paden Tolbert and Bud Ledbetter were out there in the night with five other men, biding their time until the house grew dark and quiet.

On the morning of November 30, Mrs. Harless's son appeared, walking out to fetch a bucket of water. He entered the barn and the officers snapped him up. But the boy was missed around the family hearth, and soon Mrs. Harless herself appeared and went into the barn. Ledbetter collared her and explained the situation.

They had a warrant for Jennings, said Ledbetter. He told her to go back inside and tell the outlaws that they were surrounded. Mrs. Harless delivered the message, and Ledbetter could hear sounds of argument from inside the house. Quickly Mrs. Harless left the house, swathed in blankets against the cold.

Jennings opened fire, but within a few minutes the outlaws realized it was time to flee, running out the back of the cabin, heading for an orchard, scrambling through the gunfire. They were lucky. One peace officer's rifle jammed at the first shot. A second got a charge of shot into Frank Jennings, without appreciably slowing him down. All of the bandits had been hit, but none so crippled that he could not flee on foot.

Al Jennings had been hit three times, including taking a bullet in his left thigh, but he could still move, and the bandits waded a creek and disappeared. Ledbetter was not happy when the officers lost the trail and could not pick it up again after a long search.

The fleeing gang commandeered a wagon from two Indian boys, finally holing up at the ranch of Willis Brooks. The gang may have escaped, but they were in sad shape. Al and Pat O'Malley, at least, needed medical attention, and Brooks went into Checotah, ostensibly to find a doctor.

Instead he found Bud Ledbetter and told him where the gang was hiding. That night Ledbetter, Tolbert, and two other lawmen set up an ambush in a ravine near a passing road. They dropped a tree across the road as a barricade and settled in to wait. They waited most of the night until a wagon came. Al and O'Malley were bedded down in the back and Frank was driving. Brooks had given them directions supposed to take them safely to Arkansas. In fact, he sent them straight into Ledbetter's trap. There was no fight this time. Confronted by four rifles, the outlaws gave it up and were transported to the Muskogee jail, where Morris O'Malley already languished.

Little Dick West was still free and still wanted. West had friends in the territory, so he could often find a safe place to hole up. Moreover, he had long been famous for wanting to sleep out of doors whatever the weather, someplace out in the brush away from people.

Enter Deputy US Marshal Heck Thomas, who had kept order in the territory for long years and had killed Bill Doolin when the outlaw leader would not heed his order to surrender. If anybody could run West down, it would be Thomas.

West was working as a farmhand between Kingfisher and Guthrie, laboring for two different farmers. Local farmers spilled the beans in Guthrie, saying that farmer Fitzgerald's hired hand was trying to get them to commit a robbery with him. Such evil tidings quickly found their way to Thomas. While the hired man used an alias, Thomas guessed from his description that he was hearing about Little Dick West.

Thomas led a four-man posse, which included the formidable Bill Tilghman, off to the Fitzgerald farm. Fitzgerald said he didn't know anything about the hired man who, in any event, had long since left his employ. In Fitzgerald's barn the lawmen found a horse matching the description of West's. The farmer said that he traded for the animal.

Unconvinced, the posse rode off and got lucky, spotting a man scouting along the timber. Thomas and Tilghman began to follow him, and the other three members of the posse rode on. Then they saw the same man standing by a farm shed. The man promptly stepped behind the barn and ran for it, and the three lawmen stepped into the open and ordered him to halt.

It was West, and he kept running, snapping off several shots from his revolver. The lawmen responded with shotgun and rifle fire, and West was hit as he dived under the bottom strand of a barbed-wire fence. He was dead before the posse could reach him.

With his gang either killed or in the lockup, Al Jennings could start his second career, having been a notable flop at the first one. First, though, he had to go off to prison for a while. His sentence was reduced to only five years and he received a presidential pardon.

Jennings settled in Oklahoma City in 1911, went back to practicing law, set his sights on political office, and won nomination for county attorney of Oklahoma County on the Democratic ticket. He lost in the general election, but two years later he ran for governor, of all things, openly talking about his outlaw days. By then his life on the scout was commemorated not only by his 1913 book, *Beating Back*, but also by a film of the same title. Al even starred in the movie, which at least gave him great face recognition with the voters.

It wasn't enough. The best Al could do was finish third in a field of six in the Democratic primary. He gave up both politics and the practice of law and retired to sunny California, where he went to work making Western films. He died in Tarzana, California, the day after Christmas, 1961.

It had been quite a life.

The Battle of Ingalls

Lawman Tom Speed stopped his wagon in front of Pierce's livery stable. He walked inside, threatened the owner and his stable boy with his Winchester, and advised quiet on pain of death. Up the street in Ingalls, outlaw Bitter Creek Newcomb saw the wagon halt near the livery stable. Ever wary, he decided to investigate. At the same time he would check on his horse, left for shoeing at Wagner's blacksmith shop. Finding that his mount was ready, he began to walk the horse toward the suspicious wagon.

Now Speed, spotting the horseman approaching, asked a passerby, fourteen-year-old Del Simmons, the identity of the man. Surprised, the lad blurted out, "Why, that's Bitter Creek!" Newcomb heard the exclamation, whirled to see the boy point at him, and yanked his Winchester from its scabbard.

Speed immediately pulled down on Newcomb, and his first round smashed Newcomb's rifle and tore into the outlaw's right leg and groin. Badly hurt, his rifle useless, Newcomb wheeled his horse to run, and Speed stepped clear of the building to kill him.

In his barren room at the top of the OK Hotel, gang member Arkansas Tom heard the firing. Dashing to the window with his Winchester, he spotted Tom Speed aiming at Bitter Creek Newcomb and put a bullet in the lawman's shoulder. He fired again as Speed staggered toward the cover of his wagon, and the marshal went down in the dusty street, his lungs filling with his own blood.

The war had begun too quickly, and the lawmen had been caught out of position. Over on Oak Street, the marshal's men

The OK Hotel, from which Arkansas Tom mortally wounded three law-men *Western History Collections, University of Oklahoma Libraries*

opened up on Newcomb as he galloped for safety, reeling in the saddle. A roar of gunfire erupted from Ransom's Saloon as Dynamite Dick, Doolin, Dalton, and Tulsa Jack laid down a barrage to cover their comrade.

Young Simmons ducked into Vaughn's saloon to avoid the hail of fire, but as he sprinted out the back door of the bar, a rifle bullet tore into his body. He would not live to see the night. A local salesman, rashly bolting from the back door of the saloon, took a slug in the liver, probably mistaken by the shooter for an outlaw. The bartender wisely forted up with the liquor supply, stored in a thick-walled icebox. The town drunk, a man simply named Newlin, more or less comatose, apparently missed the whole gunfight.

Out in the street Winchester bullets downed a horse belonging to town resident Neil Murray and disintegrated a chicken that chose the wrong time to cross the street. The town's residents ran for cover, mothers collecting children as the lead flew everywhere. Some citizens huddled under feather beds; others sought shelter in cellars and caves.

Dr. Duncan Selph's two small boys abandoned their precious marbles in the street and dashed for safety. Their redoubtable father did not, simply walking boldly down the street to his home. "The outlaws knew me," he later said, "so did the marshals, and I had little fear of being shot."

Now Tom Hueston led other lawmen behind the Ash Street buildings to surround the saloon. Marshal Hixon led his men west along both sides of Second Street, drew a deep breath, and shouted toward Ransom's Saloon.

"You are surrounded!" he roared. "Surrender!"

Doolin wasted no words in reply: "Go to hell!"

Hixon's response was a murderous hail of bullets that ripped through the board walls of the saloon. After the fight the bartender would count 172 holes in the building. Local sot Newlin apparently drowsed on through the whole war.

Doolin's gang had been in tight places before, but nothing like this. There could be no staying in the saloon while the lawmen reduced it to splinters. Whatever it cost, the only chance of salvation lay in flight and firepower. They were aided by a citizen, Neil Murray, who tried to draw the lawmen's attention by standing in the saloon door with a Winchester at his shoulder. Murray drew a little more attention than he really wanted, collapsing in the doorway, still alive, with three slugs in his body.

The Doolin Gang's break for safety was sudden and violent, and apparently the lawmen did not see them bolt from a shed on the south side of the saloon. In the shed the gang had stashed horses. Doolin and Dynamite Dick desperately threw saddles on the gang's mounts, while Dalton and Tulsa Jack filled the air with bullets.

As Tom Hueston and his men began to take fire from the stable, they changed position to cover that building. Hueston himself ran to a lumber pile behind the stable, intent on cutting off the flight of the outlaws, his whole attention focused on the stable. The move was his death warrant.

In the attic of the OK Hotel, Arkansas Tom Jones had knocked shingles from the roof to open a hole that gave him a clear view of the stable. Standing on a chair or some other furniture, Arkansas Tom drove a slug through Hueston's guts, and the lawman went down. He would be dead before sunset the next day.

By this time some of the other lawmen realized they were taking fire from a sniper, although they could not locate the source of the fire. They continued to hammer bullets into the stable, still trying to head off the gang's escape. Hixon himself was lying in a shallow ditch, drilling Winchester rounds at the muzzle flashes of the outlaws' rifles. Nearby, lawman Ed Masterson squeezed his body behind a little tree half as thick as he was, while bullets tore limbs and chunks from his fragile shelter.

And then as Masterson ran to the wagon for more ammunition, Doolin, Dalton, Dynamite Dick, and Tulsa Jack burst from the stable, galloping madly southwest toward a shallow draw the lawmen had left uncovered. Hixon promptly nailed Dalton's horse in the jaw, and the animal went mad.

Dalton urged the frantic horse on a little farther until a round from Lafe Shadley's rifle broke the animal's leg. Dalton then left his mount, running toward a barbed-wire fence that blocked the gang's escape. Suddenly he stopped, spun around, and ran back toward his horse to snatch from its saddlebags the gang's only set of wire cutters.

Lafe Shadley then left the shelter of a Dr. Call's house, apparently trying to get a better shot at the gang. His coat caught on a wire fence, throwing him forward. A round from Arkansas Tom's deadly Winchester smashed his right hip and glanced up into the right side of his chest.

As Shadley went down, Dalton finished cutting the fence and the gang galloped frantically down the draw and off to the southeast. Every lawman within view blazed away at them, but the range opened quickly and only one slug hit anybody. At the time the lawmen thought they had hit Dalton but would later learn that they had gotten a round into Dynamite Dick, who would survive.

Up to now Arkansas Tom had it all his own way. Now, however, the vengeful lawmen turned their full firepower on the attic of the battered OK Hotel. A torrent of fire ripped and tore at the raw wood structure. One survivor told the story this way:

> During a lull, he said, I was told . . . to go to Hotel, that
> Jones was up there either wounded or killed. . . . [H]e
> came to the top of the stairs and says "is that you Dock?"
> and I told him it was. . . . Had his Winchester in his
> hands & revolvers on the bed. I said Tom come down
> and surrender. He says "I can't do it for I won't get justice.
> . . . I don't want to hurt anyone but I won't be taken alive."

But he was. For all his tough talk, Arkansas Tom Jones lost heart when he learned the gang had abandoned him and the enraged lawmen were threatening to dynamite the hotel. He surrendered without a fight early in the afternoon. He was lucky to be alive—the room was in shambles, its walls riddled with rifle slugs, the water pitcher and the mirror shattered. The battle of Ingalls was over.

In Ingalls the stunned citizens surveyed the battered remains of their town. A few of the more insensitive found time for some crude frontier merriment before the lawmen's blood had dried in the dust. Finding town drunk Newlin asleep behind Ransom's bar, they stuffed intestines from the dead chicken down the front of his coveralls, then woke him. He awoke, still drunk, and shouted, "My god, they've shot my guts out!" Most townsfolk felt sympathy for the poor drunk but saw the humor.

The Ingalls fight sealed the fate of the Doolin Gang and of the town itself. Arkansas Tom was the first to go, duly tried and sentenced to fifty years in prison at Lansing. After years of confinement he was released, only to return to crime. Hunted for bank robbery, he died in 1924, shot down by law officers in Joplin, Missouri.

Not long after sentencing Arkansas Tom, Chief Justice Frank Dale called Marshal Evett Nix into his office and spoke plainly: "Marshal . . . I have reached the conclusion that the only good outlaw is a dead one. I hope you will instruct your deputies in the future to bring them in dead."

That suited the marshals perfectly and they hunted the Doolin Gang over a thousand square miles. After a train holdup in April 1895, a posse under Chris Madsen flushed the gang from a thicket along the Cimarron, and a local sheriff got a round

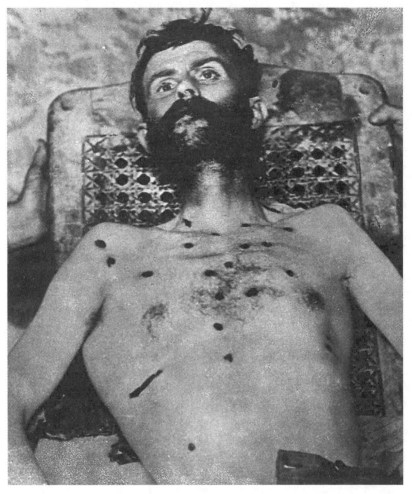

Bill Doolin, after his encounter with Heck Thomas's shotgun *Western History Collections, University of Oklahoma Libraries*

into Doolin's left foot. In another wild shootout Madsen's men killed Tulsa Jack Blake and several horses and shot a finger off "Little Bill" Raidler.

Less than a month later, Charley Pierce and Bitter Creek were killed on the Cimarron by two brothers named Dunn, probably for the reward offered for the outlaws. The Dunns, themselves no strangers to the wrong side of the law, simultane-ously forgave themselves of a debt of $900 that they owed Bitter Creek. Red Buck Waightman was killed by a posse at his Cana-dian River hideout in early 1896. Dynamite Dick Clifton lived on the run into the autumn of 1897, when a party of marshals cut him down near Checotah, Oklahoma.

Dalton, after leading a raid against a Longview, Texas, bank, went into hiding near Ardmore, Oklahoma. There, on September 25, 1895, lawmen surprised Dalton, who leaped through a back window and ran. Challenged to halt, he turned and raised his revolver. Deputy Marshal Loss Hart drove a Winchester .44 bullet through his body, and the last of the outlaw Daltons passed into history.

Doolin survived into the summer of 1896. On August 25, returning from a New Mexico refuge to collect his wife and child, he was surprised by Heck Thomas and a posse near Lawton, Oklahoma. As Doolin led his horse along a path in the darkness, Heck Thomas roared, "Halt, Bill!" Doolin reacted instantly, whipped up his Winchester to fire twice at the sound of Thomas's voice, then drew his revolver and snapped several more rounds into the gloom. Heck Thomas pulled down on the outlaw with an eight-gauge shotgun, and Doolin fell, riddled with twenty pieces of buckshot.

Doolin was buried in a Stillwater cemetery, a rusty buggy axle his only monument. The local paper commented dryly, "[H]is left leg will get a rest."

It was the end of the Wild Bunch, last of the old train-robbing, bank-busting outfits. There would be more outlaws, but the Ingalls fight marked at least the beginning of the end of unre-strained lawlessness, the dawn of more settled times.

Ingalls took longer to die. Some of its citizens tried to distance themselves from the town's tarnished reputation, passing resolutions deploring the old, bad days. Nevertheless, the press of neighboring towns continued to portray Ingalls as a lawless place, and a certain amount of violence did continue to cloud its reputation. In September 1894 Neil Murray got himself shot in a scuffle with another man, and a monumental Donnybrook was fought in the town's streets early the next year.

A leading citizen was murdered late in 1895, and before the year was out, a father-son spat ended in another shooting. Worst of all for the town's reputation, a quarrel between church factions led to the dynamiting of the Christian Church in the spring of 1901.

The kiss of death for Ingalls came, however, when the Atchison, Topeka and Santa Fe passed by to the south and left Ingalls isolated. The railroad's northbound line bent west to curve around Ingalls, running instead through rival Stillwater. Ingalls's last hope, the Katy line, ran north and south to the east of the town, and Ingalls died on the vine.

The infamous OK Hotel departed in 1901, reassembled to become Stillwater's Globe Hotel. By about the time of World War I, even Ingalls's name was gone. The site had a brief reincarnation during the discovery of oil in the area, and in 1921 a post office called Signet appeared on the site. Then Signet, too, quickly became a wraith.

In 1938 some past and present citizens of Ingalls erected a substantial monument to Marshals Speed, Hueston, and Shadley. Sadly, a truck later backed into the memorial. Though it has since been repaired, it now stands alone and a bit forlorn, with little but the wind and dust for company.

The Dalton Boys
Overrated

The night was ablaze with gunfire as a dozen rifles sounded in the streets of little Adair, Oklahoma. In the gloom the Dalton Gang galloped out of town, spraying bullets at the porch of Skinner's Store. Two unarmed men stood there watching, and both went down. That pointless assault was bad enough, but it turned out that both men were doctors, and one of them later died.

Those shots would turn every man's hand against the gang, for what passed as the code of the West dictated that you didn't molest a respectable woman, harm a preacher, or shoot physicians (who took care of everybody on both sides of the law). The gang didn't know it, but they had now sentenced themselves to destruction.

In May 1891 an outlaw band robbed a train at Wharton, a compound of two buildings near what is now Perry. This was the first job of "the Dalton Gang." As Emmett Dalton related in typically whiny prose years later, the raid was a "blind striking back at all corporate interests in any way related to their troubles." In fact, the motives were much simpler: They wanted money the easy way, and for a while things went well, although the amounts taken in their hauls were disappointing.

The gang planned their crowning achievement, the robbery of a train carrying the Sac and Fox tribal annuity, some $70,000 of it—a bonanza for the time. They would strike the train at

Red Rock. But when the night came, Bob Dalton was alarmed by the darkened appearance of the train. In Emmett's inimitable prose, he described the train as "sinister as a vault!" Bob was suspicious and correct, because the train carried a detachment of lawmen led by Wells, Fargo detective Fred Dodge, all armed to the teeth and waiting for the robbers to appear.

And so Bob and his minions waited for the next train and pounced on the express car. The express car carried a special kind of safe, a through safe: one whose keys were at the car's destination. There was also a "way safe," which contained only minor amounts of money, destined for intermediate stops along the train's route. The agent could not open the through safe; and with typical lack of planning, the gang had not thought to bring dynamite, the only possible way to crack this safe.

This haul was also relatively measly, something around $3,000, so the boys spitefully stole the train crew's small change and lunch boxes. Legend says they also stole three or four boxes of silk stockings and other female finery, all of it intended for Bob's mistress, Flo Quick; Emmett's flame, Julia Johnson; and Bitter Creek Newcomb's little inamorata, Rose Dunn.

Bob now led the gang on still another train robbery, aiming this time for the station at Pryor Creek. Spotted there by an Indian farmer, Bob changed plans. Maybe robbing the train at Adair instead of Pryor Creek would thwart the law. The plan worked, and they rode off with some cash.

The Dalton boys came from an honest family. At the age of sixteen, Adeline Younger, aunt to the formidable Younger brothers, married Lewis Dalton. Most of the Dalton offspring turned out to be good citizens, a credit to their hardworking mother.

Frank, the oldest brother, was a highly respected deputy US marshal. Frank died in action, shot down in the brakes of the Arkansas by four outlaws. There are all manner of fables about how Frank's brothers hunted down his killers, but all of these appear to be pure moonshine, part of the deep-rooted mythology that surrounds most famous outlaws. In fact, what apparently happened is that another lawman killed three of Frank's murderers, and another deputy got the fourth later on, but that retribution was cold comfort to Adeline.

The family lived for a while up in Cass County, Missouri, farming on land Adeline had inherited; brothers Bob, Grat, and Emmett were all born there. In time the family moved farther south into Indian Territory, settling at a place called Locust Hill. Adeline was in a state of more or less perpetual pregnancy, but she managed to keep her brood together and at the same time be a good neighbor and friend to those who lived nearby.

At last Adeline had enough of Lewis. Maybe divorced, maybe not, in 1890 Lewis did everybody a favor and died, and Adeline moved her brood to 160 acres of good land near Kingfisher, northwest of Oklahoma City. The neighbors thought Adeline was "as nice a little old lady as you could find anywhere, well educated and interesting to talk to."

Despite Adeline's sweetness Bob, Grat, and Emmett grew up tough. Both Grat and Emmett had reputations as formidable fistfighters; Grat was a budding alcoholic; and Bob was famous for his prowess with a rifle, said to have been able to hit a tomato can in the air three times before it reached the ground.

Early on, Grat and Bob worked as lawmen for both the US marshal and the Osage Indian police. Life as a lawman seems to have been too tame—or unrewarding—for the brothers, and they turned to horse thievery, stealing at least three herds and peddling them over the Kansas border in Baxter Springs.

The brothers left Baxter Springs in a hurry after the last horse theft. Grat may even have spent a few weeks in jail there, while Bob and Emmett drifted west to safe climes. These safer climes were New Mexico, specifically the wild town of Santa Rosa, where the brothers went with future gang members Black-Faced Charley Bryant and Bitter Creek Newcomb, and somebody who called himself, somewhat obscurely, the "Narrow-Gauge Kid." They stole and pillaged their way through parts of New Mexico, eventually winding up back in Oklahoma.

For a while they hid at a place near Hennessey, a "love nest," which Bob shared with a seductive lady called Eugenia Moore, who may have been Flo Quick. No matter who she was, she's said to have acted as a spy when the gang started robbing trains, sweet-talking station agents and keeping one pearly ear cocked for the clatter of the telegraph announcing money shipments.

But the land was changing, and there would be less and less room for outlaws, especially those who stepped over the line and murdered doctors. Bob could see trouble coming and resolved to clear out. But for that they needed a grubstake, and so he led his men north toward their old hometown, Coffeyville, Kansas.

The End of the Dalton Gang
Bloodbath at Coffeyville

A pair of housepainters bailed off their scaffolding and hit the ground running, and women shooed their children indoors, while the hammer of rifle fire shattered the morning calm of little Coffeyville, Kansas, just across the Oklahoma border. Three men came sprinting out of the front door of the Condon Bank, running desperately for an alley across the plaza where their horses were tethered. As they ran, dust puffed from their clothing as rifle bullets tore into their bodies. What had seemed an easy payday had turned into disaster.

The outlaws rode in from the west through a crisp, brilliant October morning in 1892, a little group of five dusty young men. They laughed and joked together, enjoying the lovely autumn morning. Three of them were Daltons, and they knew the town, or thought they did, because they had lived nearby. They felt the town was a perfect target; nobody carried a gun anymore, including the town marshal.

Their leader, cocky Bob Dalton, had a plan and boasted that the Dalton Gang would do what no outlaws had ever done before: They would rob two banks—the Condon and the First National—at once. It would be a feat never managed even by their famous cousins, the Younger boys, now languishing in a Minnesota prison, or by those boon companions of the Youngers, Frank and Jesse James.

The Condon Bank in Coffeyville, where the staff bamboozled Grat Dalton
Western History Collections, University of Oklahoma Libraries

The Dalton Gang, lined up for their obligatory last photo in a Coffeyville alley *Western History Collections, University of Oklahoma Libraries*

Backing the brothers were two experienced members of the gang, Dick Broadwell and Bill Powers. Grat led Powers and Broadwell into the Condon. Emmett and Bob went on across the street to the First National. Inside, the robbers threw down on customers and employees and began to direct the bankers to deliver each bank's money and be damn quick about it.

What they did not know was that somebody, probably a storekeeper who had known the family, recognized one of the brothers as they crossed the plaza. He spread the word that the dreaded Daltons were in town, and citizens began to search about for weapons.

Next door to the First National, Isham's Hardware looked out on the front door of the Condon and into the plaza, and thence down the narrow alley where the gang left its horses. Isham's and another hardware store nearby started handing out weapons to anybody who wanted them, and more than a dozen public-spirited citizens armed themselves.

Inside the Condon dense Grat Dalton started out by collecting a prodigious pile of silver, so heavy that it would take more than one man to carry it. After that, he was bamboozled by a courageous young employee, Charley Ball. Ball looked the outlaw square in the eye and blandly announced that the time lock to the vault (that had opened long before) would not unlock for several minutes. "Eight minutes," crowed a later newspaper report, "was the time consumed by Cashier Ball in his one-act skit of 'the Bogus Time Lock.'"

That eight minutes saved the bank treasure and cost the Dalton Gang its existence. While Ball courageously told Grat Dalton this colossal fib, another employee helpfully rattled the vault doors to complete the illusion. Instead of trying those doors himself, Grat stood stupidly and waited for the hands of the clock to move, while outside the townsmen loaded Winchesters and found cover.

About the time Grat began to suspect that he was being had, somebody outside fired at his brothers as they emerged from the First National. Bob and Emmett had gotten a sackful of cash, in spite of the bankmen's deliberate foot dragging. The brothers finished their looting, collected some hostages, and pushed out the door into the plaza, but when somebody took a shot at them, they dove back into the First National and ran out the back door, where Bob shot down one local man. The two kept going, circling around through a side street, out of sight of the waiting citizens.

Bullets began to shatter the windows of the Condon Bank, and one tore into Broadwell's left arm. Grat, Broadwell, and

Powers could not match the firepower of the locals, as some two hundred projectiles of various sizes slammed into the windows.

One defender at Isham's was hit in the chest by their return fire and knocked flat—but all he got from the outlaw bullet was a bruised chest, for the slug hit an iron spanner in his shirt pocket and did him no permanent damage.

The townsmen's heavy and accurate fire convinced Grat that it was high time to go. Leaving behind the enormous heap of coins, the three outlaws charged out into the plaza, straight into the line of fire of the rifles at the hardware store, running hard for their horses, now so very far away down the alley. There was no cover, and it must have seemed as if everybody in town was shooting at them.

Grat could have led the way around the corner, out of sight of that deadly nest of riflemen at Isham's in just a couple of strides, or he could have sought the bank's back door. Instead, Grat led his men out into the plaza, directly into the killing zone, running hard for the alley and firing at the shooters inside Isham's Hardware. All three outlaws were hit before they reached their horses. Witnesses saw dust puff from their clothing as rifle bullets tore into them.

Meanwhile, Bob and Emmett came out of the alley behind the First National and got behind some townsmen still facing down the street toward the First National and the Condon. Bob shot an armed shoemaker in the back. An older man, a Civil War veteran and also a cobbler, courageously reached for the fallen man's rifle, but Bob killed him too. He then drove a round through the cheek of still another citizen, and then the outlaw brothers ran on, trying to get to Grat and the horses.

Grat and the others, wounded and staggering, got to their horses about when the town marshal, Charles Connelly, appeared from another direction. Connelly miscalculated the position of the fleeing outlaws and came between them and their horses. Grat shot the lawman down from behind, and then liveryman John Kloehr, the town's best shot, put Grat down for good with a bullet in the neck.

About this time someone nailed Bob Dalton, who slumped down on a pile of cobblestones. Still game, he kept on working his Winchester and fired several aimless shots, one of which slammed harmlessly into a box of dynamite over at Isham's. Kloehr drove a bullet into Bob's chest and finished him. The outlaw leader slumped over on his side and died in the alley. Powers lay dead in the dust about ten feet away.

Broadwell, mortally wounded, still managed to get to his horse and ride half a mile toward safety before he pitched out of his saddle, dead in the road. Young Emmett, still carrying the grain sack of loot from the First National, miraculously managed to get mounted. He jerked his horse back into the teeth of the citizens' fire, reaching down from the saddle for his dying brother Bob. But just then Carey Seaman, the town barber, blew Emmett out of the saddle with both barrels of his shotgun. The fight was over.

Four citizens were dead. Three more were wounded. The man with a rifle slug through one cheek was expected to die. Four bandits had also died, and Emmett was punched full of more than twenty bullet holes. He was carried up to the second-floor office of Dr. Wells, who set out to save the young outlaw's life if he could.

While the doctor was at work, a group of citizens, angry at the death of four of their fellows, appeared in the doctor's office carrying a rope. The idea was to tie one end to a telegraph pole outside the doctor's window, attach the other end to Emmett, and throw him out the window. "No use, boys," said the doctor. "He will die anyway."

"Are you sure, doc?" said a voice from the crowd.

"Yes," said Doc Wells, "did you ever hear of a patient of mine getting well?" That broke the tension and at last cooler heads prevailed. Emmett was saved, preserved for trial and a long spell in the Kansas state penitentiary.

After the custom of the time, the four expired bandits were propped up both vertically and horizontally to have their pictures taken. People came from far and near to see the corpses and collect souvenirs: bits of bloody cloth, hairs from the dead horses, and so on. Some brought the kids, it being thought that the edifying sight of dead bandits was helpful in keeping the young on the path of righteousness. Some sightseers indulged in a somewhat macabre experiment in hydraulics; somebody discovered that if you worked Grat Dalton's arm up and down like a pump handle, blood squirted out of the hole in his throat.

So the rifles at the hardware store, and John Kloehr, and Carey Seaman, had accounted for all the bandits, except one. Emmett always said there were only five bandits involved in the raid. However, four sober, respectable townsfolk, the Hollingsworths and the Seldomridges, said they passed six riders heading into town on the morning of the raid, although nobody else who saw the raiders thought there were more than five. Two days after the fight, David Stewart Elliott, editor of the *Coffeyville Journal* and the only reliable historian of the raid, had this to say: "It is supposed the sixth man was too well-known to risk coming into the heart of the city, and that he kept off some distance and watched the horses."

Later, in *Last Raid of the Daltons*, Elliott did not mention a sixth rider, although in his book he used much of the text of his newspaper story. Maybe he had talked again to the Seldomridges and Hollingsworths, and maybe they had told him they could not be certain there were six riders. Maybe, but still another citizen also said more than five bandits attacked Coffeyville.

Many years later, Tom Babb, one of the courageous Condon Bank employees, told a reporter that he had seen a sixth man gallop out of the alley where the horses were stashed. The man rode away from that deadly plaza, he said, turned south, and disappeared.

If Tom Babb saw anything, it might have been Bitter Creek Newcomb, one of several nominees for Sixth Man. He was a veteran gang member, said to have been left out of the raid because he was given to loose talk. One story has Bitter Creek riding in from the south "to support the gang from a different angle." If he did, Babb might have seen him from the Condon's windows, which faced south.

However, the most popular candidate was always Bill Doolin, who in 1896 told several lawmen he rode along on the raid. No further questioning was ever possible, because in 1896 Doolin shot it out with the implacable Heck Thomas and came in second. A whole host of writers supported Doolin's tale. His horse went lame, the story goes, and Doolin turned aside to catch another mount, arriving in town too late to help his comrades. The obvious trouble with this theory is that neither Bob Dalton nor any other bandit leader would have attacked his objective shorthanded instead of waiting a few minutes for one of his best guns to steal a new horse.

Nevertheless, the Doolin enthusiasts theorized that Doolin had gotten his new horse and was on his way to catch up with the gang when he met a citizen riding furiously to warn the countryside. The man stopped to ask Doolin if he had met any bandits. Doolin cleverly said he hadn't and, ever resourceful, added:

> Holy smoke! I'll just wheel around right here and go on ahead of you down this road and carry the news. Mine is a faster horse than yours. Doolin then started on a ride that has ever since been the admiration of horsemen in the Southwest. . . . Doolin . . . crossed the Territory like a flying wraith . . . a ghostly rider saddled upon the wind.

The "flying wraith" fable is much repeated, and that language—and the part about a ghostly rider on the wind—is certainly evocative. One writer says Doolin "never stopped" until he reached sanctuary "west of Tulsa," a phenomenal distance.

But before anybody dismisses Doolin as the sixth bandit, there's another piece of evidence. Fred Dodge, an experienced Wells, Fargo agent, stuck to the Daltons like a burr on a dogie. He was with Deputy Marshal Heck Thomas, only about a day behind the gang on the day of the raid.

Dodge wrote later that an informant said Doolin rode with the other five bandits on the way to Coffeyville, but that on the day of the raid, he was ill with dengue fever. Although Heck Thomas remembered they received information that there were five men in the gang, Dodge had no reason to invent the informant. And, if Dodge's information was accurate, Doolin's dengue fever would explain his dropping out just before the raid a great deal better than the fable about a lame horse.

Not everybody agreed on Doolin or Bitter Creek as the mystery rider. After the raid some newspapers reported the culprit was one Allee Ogee, variously reported as hunted, wounded, and killed. Ogee, as it turned out, was very much alive, and industriously pursuing his job in a Wichita packinghouse. Understandably irritated, Ogee wrote the *Coffeyville Journal*, announcing both his innocence and his continued existence.

A better candidate is yet another Dalton, brother Bill, lately moved from California with wrath in his heart for banks and railroads. Obnoxious Bill had few scruples about robbing or shooting people; after Coffeyville he rode with Doolin's dangerous gang and finally set up as a gang leader on his own.

Before Bill Dalton was shot down trying to escape a deputy marshal, as far as anybody knows, he said nothing about being at Coffeyville, and afterward he couldn't comment, being quite dead. So nothing concrete connects Bill Dalton with story of the sixth rider, except his perpetually surly disposition, his propensity for the crooked life, and his association with his outlaw brothers.

In later years Deputy Marshal Chris Madsen commented on the Coffeyville raid for Frank Latta's excellent *Dalton Gang Days*. If what Madsen said was true, neither Doolin nor Bill Dalton could have been the sixth bandit. Madsen was in Guthrie when the Coffeyville raid came unraveled, was advised of its results by telegram, and forthwith told the press. Almost immediately, he said, Bill Dalton appeared to ask whether the report was true. Madsen believed that Bill and Doolin both were near Guthrie, waiting for the rest of the gang with fresh horses. You have to respect anything Madsen said, although some writers have suggested that the tough Dane was not above making a fine story even better. We'll never know.

Other men have also been nominated as the One Who Got Away, among them a mysterious outlaw called Buckskin Ike, rumored to have ridden with the Dalton Gang in happier times. And there was one Padgett, a yarn spinner of the "I bin everwhar" persuasion. Padgett later bragged that he left whiskey running in the Cherokee Nation to ride with the Daltons. At Coffeyville he was the appointed horse holder, he said, and rode for his life when things began to come unstuck in that deadly alley.

Some have suggested that the sixth rider might even have been a woman, an unlikely but intriguing theory. Stories abound about the Dalton women, in particular Eugenia Moore, Julia Johnson, and the Rose of Cimarron. The Rose was said to be an Ingalls, Oklahoma, girl, who loved Bitter Creek Newcomb.

And then there was Julia Johnson, whom Emmett married in 1907. Emmett wrote that he had been smitten by Julia long before the raid, when he stopped to investigate organ music coming from a country church. Entering the building, he discovered Julia in the bloom of young womanhood, playing the organ. It was love at first sight for them both. Well, maybe so, although Julia's granddaughter later said that Julia couldn't play a lick, let alone generate angelic chords from the church organ.

Julia, Emmett said, was the soul of constancy and waited patiently for her outlaw lover through all the long years in prison. Never mind that Julia married two other people, who both departed this life due to terminal lead poisoning. Never mind that she married her second husband while Emmett was in the pen. The myth of maidenly devotion is too well entrenched to die.

Julia has been proposed as the sixth rider more than once, without any real foundation in fact. However, aside from the fact that Julia probably never laid eyes on Emmett until he left prison—that's what her granddaughter said, anyway—there's no evidence Julia rode on any Dalton raid, let alone the failed attack on the Coffeyville banks.

Eugenia Moore was the mysterious lady supposed to be Bob's inamorata and spy. It was she who rode boldly up and down the railroad between Texas and Kansas, seducing freight agents and eavesdropping on the telegraph for news of money shipments (oh, yes, she was a telegrapher, too). Eugenia might have been Flo Quick, a real-life horse thief. When she rode out to steal, she dressed as a man and called herself "Tom King." The *Wichita Daily Eagle* rhapsodized: "She is an elegant rider, very daring. She has . . . eyes like sloes that would tempt a Knight of St. John. . . . [H]er figure is faultless."

Even if the reporter overdid it a little, Flo was no doubt a very attractive, charming woman. So maybe she was really Bob Dalton's mistress. If she was, she might have ridden along on the raid, although there is no evidence whatever to place her there.

Who really was a sixth bandit, if there was one? Maybe he was somebody relatively unknown, maybe Padgett or somebody like him, but that is unlikely. This was to be a big raid, the pot of gold at the end of Bob Dalton's rainbow. He would not take along anybody but a proven, experienced gang member, not even to hold the horses for the rest of the outlaws.

Doolin remains the leading candidate, and there is substantial evidence supporting his candidacy. Even so I'm inclined to bet on Bill Dalton, in spite of Chris Madsen's story. There is no direct evidence to indicate he rode to Coffeyville with the rest, but he may well have gathered intelligence for the gang before they rode north to Kansas, and he certainly turned to the owl hoot trail in a hurry after Coffeyville. He was violent and without scruple, and he loathed what he considered the Establishment: banks and railroads.

Was there a sixth bandit at all? There's one bit of tantalizing information, a haunting reference that seems never to have been followed up and now can never be. In 1973 an elderly Coffeyville woman reminisced about the bloody end of the raid: "Finally they got on their horses . . . those that were left. Several of 'em of course, were killed there, as well as several of the town's people. And they got on their horses and left."

So passed the Daltons, in one of the most famous and disastrous holdups in Western outlaw history. Bob and Grat are still in Coffeyville, up in the cemetery. They have a headstone these days, but planted alongside it is a piece of ordinary pipe. For many years it was their only monument, and it is surely the most enduring one.

It's the pipe to which they tied their horses in Death Alley.

The Two Faces of Ned Christie

Deputy US Marshal Dan Maples, a well-respected lawman, was in Indian Territory searching for outlaws. He and his small posse—which included his young son Sam—camped close to the Big Spring, a plentiful source of water. Maples and a posse man went into town for supplies and, on the way back, walked into an ambush. It happened as they were crossing Spring Branch Creek, using a log that served as a bridge.

Posseman Jefferson, in the lead, saw somebody's shiny revolver in a thicket ahead. The holder of the revolver fired twice, and Maples went down. He managed to pull his revolver and fire four times into the thicket, but the attacker vanished. Officers investigating the murder scene soon found a black coat with a bullet hole in it, what was left of a whiskey bottle in the pocket.

Maples died the next day, and at least one local citizen's life would never be the same. Ned Christie's existence in Oklahoma was about to become news.

Over the years a great deal of chatter has abounded over Ned Christie as a career outlaw, and most tales paint him as a wanton killer. Consider this passage from the WPA *Writers' Project* back in 1938.

> Eleven murders were credited to Christie. Among his victims were two officers, an Indian woman and a half-breed boy. He was born a killer, cold blooded, ruthless; no one knew when or where he would strike next. . . . [A]long the isolated paths to the lonely cabins of settlers he stalked relentless in his maniacal hatred.

Christie was a Cherokee, described as a tall, lean, good-looking man who wore his hair long in the old tribal fashion. He came from a well-known, respected family; he was one of the sons of Watt Christie, an expert blacksmith who came west sometime in the 1830s to settle in the Goingsnake District of the Cherokee Nation.

Watt was an active, successful farmer who also carried on the smithing trade. He had several wives, a common and legal practice. Watt's extended family eventually produced eleven children, seven boys and four girls . . . or maybe it was twenty-one, depending on what account you read.

Ned was deeply bitter over the encroachment of white immigrants into the Cherokee Nation, the advance of the railroads, the planned allotment of parcels of land to individual Cherokees, and increasing agitation for statehood for the entire territory. He certainly opposed all of these things as a violation of Cherokee sovereignty, and he did not mince words about his position.

Thus far he had been a peaceful man, save for a charge of killing a young Cherokee, of which he was acquitted. But because of the events on the dark night near Big Spring, now he was suspected of the murder of Deputy US Marshal Maples, a well-known veteran federal officer.

Maples and a small posse were camped close to Tahlequah, the Cherokee capital. Whatever Maples's mission, it appeared to be fairly routine, at least as routine as any job the marshals had to do. The territory was dangerous country, where any lawman was at risk. In the end more than sixty deputy marshals would die in the line of duty in this wild area, described by a newspaper of the time as the "rendezvous of the vile and wicked from everywhere."

Ned Christie, last pose *Western History Collections, University of Oklahoma Libraries*

At the time of the murder, Christie was in Tahlequah. As a tribal legislator he had come to attend a special meeting of the Cherokee Council. The Cherokee National Female Seminary had burned down, and that tragedy had deprived the Nation of both a handsome building and the venue for the free education of young Cherokee women. The council met in emergency session to decide what action to take to replace their school.

The marshals arrested one John Parris, who lived in a disreputable part of Tahlequah called Dog Town and had spent some time on the wrong side of the law. Parris is variously described as a drinking companion or an accomplice of Christie in the Maples murder. After his arrest the hunt for Ned Christie began.

Christie and Parris were probably together on the evening of the shooting and ended up in Dog Town. That evening, according to one account, Parris and Christie left a friend's house very drunk. That was not long before Marshal Maples was murdered nearby.

In the most reliable version of what happened that night, Parris and Christie met three other Indian men. One of the three was the egregiously bad Bub Trainor, and one of the others had seen the inside of a federal prison at least twice.

A story later surfaced that another man had watched in the darkness as Bub Trainor had stolen Christie's coat as he had slept, then worn it to cut down the marshal. That same tale asserts that the dying Maples's return fire tore through Christie's coat and knocked the neck from a whiskey bottle in the pocket. Christie had bought a bottle of moonshine from Nancy Shell, who ran a Tahlequah bootleg joint, and the bottle in his coat was still plugged with a piece of Nancy's apron, torn off as a makeshift stopper. That bit of glass and strip of apron were damning evidence against Christie.

Christie woke the next day to find himself one of the suspects in the killing of Maples. Also on the short list of murderers were Parris, Parris's brother, and two other Cherokee men. All of them had been spotted near the creek at about the time of the murder. Nancy Shell identified the scrap of cloth that plugged the broken bottle's neck. She also admitted that she had sold the bottle to Christie and Parris.

Christie might have come in and surrendered to stand trial in Fort Smith, but he chose to stay away from the town. According to one tale he wanted to turn himself in, but others convinced him that he should run. In another story Christie sent a messenger to Fort Smith, asking district judge Isaac Parker to set bail, something Parker could hardly do for a man accused of the ambush murder of a federal officer.

In September 1889 veteran Deputy Marshal Heck Thomas led a serious attempt to arrest Christie. He took a posse of four men, including Deputy Marshal L. P. Isbel out of Vinita. The lawmen managed to avoid Christie's watchers, moving in slowly at night, until Christie's house was surrounded. Then Christie's dogs started barking, and the fight was on.

Christie fired from a loft window while his wife and son reloaded his rifle and pistols and handed them up to him. In an effort to break the stalemate, the posse set fire to Christie's gun shop near the house. But as Isbel leaned out from behind a tree, Christie drilled him through the right shoulder. The marshal went down, badly hurt, and Thomas hurried to help Isbel, fixing a temporary dressing around the wound.

As the flames from Christie's shop spread through the brush around the house, Christie's wife ran from the house, followed by his son, then Christie himself. Thomas fired on the fleeing figures through the smoke, putting a bullet through the younger Christie's lung. Christie himself took a round from Thomas's rifle. It smashed into his temple, tore out his right eye, and ripped loose much of the structure of the nasal bones. Christie kept going, however, and vanished into the woods. Thomas and two of his posse men briefly looked for their quarry, but Isbel was badly wounded, and Thomas's most pressing task was getting him back to medical help at Fort Smith.

Christie, Christie's son, and Isbel would all recover from their wounds. Isbel's arm was paralyzed, however, and he bid good-bye to the marshal service. Christie was terribly disfigured, no longer the handsome man he had been. From that day forward, deeply bitter, he spoke no word of English but conversed entirely in Cherokee.

Christie's kin and his friends improved his fortifications while he recovered from his terrible wound. The new lair was not far from his old home but this time was built within a rock formation on a hill that afforded good views in every direction. The rock formed a thick wall that no bullet could possible pierce.

Christie was undisturbed for a while, because it was obvious that only a very strong posse had any chance to root him out. Some people thought it would take US troops. And in the interim Christie rebuilt his home on a new site, strategically close to a spring. The new place would be called Ned's Fort. The walls were two parallel lines of logs, the space between the logs filled with sand. The walls inside were lined with oak, giving even more protection against rifle bullets. Upstairs there were no windows, only firing ports for defense.

Christie finished his new place in 1891, and a little while later the law tried again. This time the leader was an experienced deputy marshal named Dave Rusk. Rusk was a one-time Confederate officer and a crack shot. He had been a lawman for more than fifteen years when he set off to besiege Christie.

He chose a posse composed mostly of Cherokees who were not well disposed toward Christie, but his first try at Ned's Fort ended in fiasco with four of his Indian posse men wounded. For the moment he retired, but Rusk was tough and persistent. He would come again.

Rusk was back on the hunt in October of 1892. This time he led five other deputy marshals, but again the mission ended in failure. Rusk called to Christie to give up, which may have been a mistake. For Christie answered the challenge to surrender with a gobbling sound one writer called the "Cherokee death cry" and gunfire, and two deputy marshals went down, badly wounded.

Now several women and children ran out of Ned's Fort, and they told the lawmen that not only was Christie inside the fortress, but also three other Cherokee men. Rusk looked about for a better solution than going head-on against this bulletproof house. He found his answer in a rickety wagon, which the lawmen soon filled with brush and logwood. They set fire to it and then rolled it flaming into the side of the fort, hoping to burn Christie out. Trouble was, the battered wagon disintegrated on contact with the log wall, and the fire went out before it could do major damage.

Their next weapon was several sticks of dynamite lashed together. The fuse was lit and one of the posse threw the package against the side of Christie's lair. As the dynamite struck the wall, however, the fuse fell loose, and so that attempt fizzled out. Now the deputies sent a messenger into Tahlequah with instructions to wire headquarters at Fort Smith for more help. The rest of the lawmen returned to their futile siege of the log building. In the end they ran out of ammunition and had to retreat.

Another expedition against Ned's Fort was led by Paden Tolbert, a tough, experienced deputy marshal. Tolbert talked the matter over with US Marshal Jacob Yoes and Judge Parker and quietly recruited four more men, plus a fifth man to cook for the posse. Even their initial meeting was held in the dead of night. Nobody was going to take a chance that some early warning might reach Christie.

The next day the group took the train to Fort Smith, where they met John Tolbert, Paden's brother, and five more men. The group then met up with three more posse members, including Sam Maples, young son of the dead deputy marshal. One version of the fight that followed has Christie besieged by no fewer than twenty-seven posse men.

And the posse acquired an unusual piece of crime-fighting equipment. It was a small cannon, about four feet long, with forty rounds to go with it.

Other lawmen joined the posse before it moved west across the Arkansas, including Heck Bruner, one of the best of the deputy marshals, and the experienced Will Smith, who was part Cherokee. The posse now numbered about twenty-five men, and Cherokee sheriff Ben Knight—no partisan of Christie—agreed to guide them into the heart of Christie's lair.

Logically, Christie should have known this small army was coming. The lawmen could not move rapidly, and there could be no hiding so many armed men and a mule-drawn wagon loaded with a cannon and heaps of supplies from the vigilant eyes in Christie country.

The trip in was uneventful, however, and shortly after nightfall the party reached a spot behind a ridge not far from their target. Dinner was tinned sardines and crackers, for the lawmen did not build a fire. In spite of the size of their force, they still had some hope that their approach had gone undetected.

About four o'clock the next morning, the lawmen moved to their positions. Tolbert, Rusk, and two others moved the wagon to the point they had selected to get the cannon into position. With the little gun ready to fire across a creek in front of Ned's Fort, the law was ready.

About daybreak a man carrying a water bucket emerged from the cabin and headed toward the spring. Tolbert shouted to the figure to surrender, but the man dropped the bucket and dove back inside the house.

Tolbert shouted again. He is said to have told Christie they were prepared to stay this time until Christie was taken, and that he had no means of escape. Nothing happened. Then Tolbert shouted to Christie to send out any women and children who were inside the cabin. In response, three Cherokee women and a child emerged from the cabin door. Cherokee lawman Knight asked one of them who was inside helping Christie, but the women would not speak.

Now Tolbert tried again, yelling to the cabin that the posse would not leave until Christie was captured or dead. The answer was gunfire. The battle continued as the morning wore away, and gradually a group of onlookers began to form. Among them was Christie's father, Watt. Ben Knight went to Watt and asked him to help persuade his son to surrender. The father refused.

The lawmen turned to the little cannon, loaded it with black powder and something called a "bullet-wedge" projectile, and opened fire. But the heavy log walls held up through thirty-seven rounds, dented and splintered but still intact. With only three rounds left, Tolbert tried doubling the powder charge, but all that accomplished was splitting the barrel of the cannon. Night was falling by now, and Tolbert began to send his men back to camp in pairs for something to eat.

He began to explore other ways to get into the fort. His eye lit on the rear axle of the wagon that had disintegrated during the earlier siege. It was still intact. He sent men to Christie's own sawmill then, and they brought back heavy boards and used them to build a rolling barricade atop the axle, a sort of mobile shield to cover an approach to Christie's fort. The thing would be guided by the tongue of the destroyed wagon, used as a sort of lever to push the structure near the building.

The plan was for Charlie Copeland, an officer, to carry an explosive charge, six sticks of dynamite, advancing behind the shield as three more officers pushed it toward the cabin with the remaining officers providing covering fire. When they got near enough, Copeland would dash to the cabin wall and place his charge of dynamite against it.

And so, about midnight, four officers rolled the oak shield close to the logs of the cabin wall. As planned, Copeland placed the dynamite, lit the fuse, and sprinted back to the protection of the shield. They pulled the shield back a safe distance as the fuse smoked and sputtered.

A colossal blast caved in the wall of the fort and knocked over a stove inside. Now fire followed the explosion, and by dawn great gouts of flame were shooting up from the structure, garish against the coming light. Gunfire from the fort had died away. All the posse had to do was simply wait.

With one side of his fortress blown out and flames enveloping the cabin, Christie had no options left. Out of the fire and smoke, he ran suddenly, a pistol in each hand, gobbling his war cry and firing on the marshals hidden behind trees and logs and rocks. He must have known he was running to his death, charging straight ahead into those flaming rifles. And, in fact, he overran lawman Wess Bowman, who was lying on the ground. Bowman simply rolled over and shot Christie in the back of the head as he ran by.

The rest of the posse closed in then, holding their fire, but young Sam Maples ran up to empty two revolvers into what remained of Christie. The marshal's son had waited a long time to avenge his father.

An enterprising photographer emerged from the crowd of spectators and took everybody's picture. The lawmen hauled Christie's body into town and thence to Fayetteville, where everybody, the living and the dead, was loaded on the Fort Smith train. At various points Christie was propped up to take the usual photographs. In one of them somebody laid a Winchester across his folded arms. The posse also had their pictures taken again, and there was general rejoicing at the fall of a man most white people thought was Lucifer incarnate.

Not so among the Cherokee Nation. Many people, especially fellow Keetoowahs, saw the fallen man as a hero who had resisted the encroachment of the white man's law. He was admired for his courage as well. Watt Christie claimed his son's body and returned it to a family burying ground near Rabbit Trap.

So passed Ned Christie, both vilified and canonized by reams of prose of greater or lesser accuracy. His story was powerful fodder for any number of writers, some of whom were not above making up a "fact" or two to beautify their tale. Other more reliable authors simply uncritically accepted the original story that Christie cold-bloodedly shot down Marshal Maples from ambush.

The notion that Christie had murdered Maples was badly shaken when, in 1922, an elderly blacksmith came forward to insist that Christie was innocent. He had seen Christie lying on the ground drunk, he said, and watched Bub Trainor pull Christie's coat from him. The blacksmith, Dick Humphrey, somehow suspected dirty work and hid to watch what happened next. And he saw Trainor talk to Parris, then check his own revolvers, and head toward the log bridge across the little creek.

Why didn't Humphrey come forward? Because Trainor had a great many friends among the outlaw fraternity, he said, and even after Trainor was shot down a few years later, Humphrey was still afraid to speak. Only as an old man did he decide to tell his tale to a newspaper in Tulsa. Christie was, probably, innocent and became a hunted man only because of the lies Parris told the lawmen to save his own skin, plus the damning evidence of the coat with its hole and whiskey bottle's neck.

And so ended the saga of Ned Christie, hero or villain, wrongfully accused victim or callous murderer. Leaving aside the myths and legends, one thing is certain: Christie was a very tough cookie indeed, an exceptionally brave fighting man, a dead shot, and a man of conviction.

Henry Starr
More Banks than Any Other
Man in America

Ex-marshal Floyd Wilson was riding with a fellow detective, hot on the trail of a budding outlaw known as Henry Starr. Unfortunately, the second detective had fallen some distance behind Wilson when the lawman rode up on his quarry. Alone and unsure just how dangerous this new outlaw might be, the lawman pulled his Winchester out of the saddle scabbard and shouted to Starr, "Hold up. I have a warrant for you."

Starr dismounted and drew his own rifle, yelling to Wilson he should be the one to hold up, and both men opened fire at a range of only about thirty yards. Wilson probably fired first, although that shot may have been simply a warning. In his usual whiny manner, Starr later asserted that he had "pleaded with him not to make me kill him, but he opened fire, the first ball breaking my saddle and two others passing close by."

In fact, the officer's rifle jammed after that single round, and Starr shot him down. Wilson pulled his pistol as he lay on the ground, but Starr shot him again, and then once more, and finally drove a third round point-blank into Wilson's chest. The last round pierced Wilson's heart. Starr turned away from the fallen officer, whose clothing still smoldered from the muzzle blast of Starr's rifle, swung up on Wilson's horse, and rode away. Starr's outlaw career was off with a bang.

Starr was related by marriage to Belle Starr, the Bandit Queen, much celebrated in print and celluloid. Though Belle was one of the West's most enduring legends, she was no queen, and she was also one of history's all-time overrated criminals. But Henry himself was the real thing, all wool and a yard wide; the papers called him the Bearcat, but his real name truly was Henry Starr.

Through the years Starr gained a reputation as the country's greatest bank robber. When he started taking other people's money, the outlaw's favorite means of escape was the horse; by the time he finished his crooked career, he and the rest of America's robbers were carrying off their loot in automobiles.

Henry Starr was part Cherokee, born in Fort Gibson, Indian Territory, in December 1873. His father was George Starr, called "Hop," son of notorious old Tom Starr and brother to Sam Starr, the husband of the celebrated Belle. His mother, Mary Scott, was a much-respected lady. Starr got what he described as a sixth-grade education, then entered the hard adult world of work and choices.

Henry Starr did some plowing and cow punching for a while, then graduated to stealing horses. He apparently considered himself something of a free spirit, born of the Cherokee lands, not a man ever to be constrained by mere laws. As he himself told a Kansas newspaper:

> It was God overhead and nothing around. The world, our world, was ours and none to dispute. . . . We had been taught that it was ours, to have and to hold so long as grass grew and water ran, ours to hunt on, ours in which to follow in the footsteps of our fathers, to do with as we wished.

Henry Starr, where he belonged
Western History Collections, University of Oklahoma Libraries

Although he fancied himself an unfettered soul, or maybe because he did, Starr was given to blaming other people for his own shortcomings. And he blamed quite a lot of them: his stepfather, his boss, a lying witness, peace officers he said were venal and crooked, even what he called the bloody and corrupt federal court at Fort Smith.

He said, for example, that as a youngster, on his way to the site appointed for tribal payments, somebody he didn't know asked him to carry a valise to the place. Later, again according to him, deputy US marshals stopped him and found whiskey in the bag. He was, he said, badly mistreated by the lawmen, feeling the "murder-breeding leg-irons and chains." "Let any young man of ambition," he declaimed, "be shackled to a worthless perjurer and be carried 200 miles away from home, all the time being pointed out as a horse thief, to face a charge for which there is no iota of evidence . . . and what respect would he have for a law with such representatives?"

All of these people and entities, as Starr believed, drove him to a life of crime. Starr's whiny self-justification predictably excused his passage down the paths of unrighteousness, straight to a long career stealing other people's money, beginning in the summer of 1892 when he started out robbing a country store with a couple of second-rate hoodlums for backup.

He also stuck up the railway station at little Nowata, in company with career thugs Ed Newcomb and Jesse Jackson. As so often happened with Starr's confederates, however, the law quickly caught up with his cohorts: Newcomb served a long prison sentence, and Jackson killed himself in jail. Starr got away.

With practice Starr got pretty good at larceny, and he raised his sights. In December of that year, he visited Coffeyville, Kansas, where he bought wire cutters and gun holsters, in preparation for greater things. Starr apparently saw nothing wrong in jumping bail after one of his early crimes, leaving people who believed in him holding the bag, nor did his conscience seem to bother him when he hid out at the home of a friend and then stole the friend's money, about $300, a substantial nest egg.

Floyd Wilson was probably the only man Starr ever killed, but that was hardly due to Starr's peaceable nature. The outlaw surely did a lot of pistol waving in his robbing days, and a good deal of indiscriminate shooting as well. Fortunately for the general public, he never hit anybody else, unless he did some quiet murdering that is not recorded.

Despite the outright murder of Wilson, Starr the outlaw started slow. Much of his early robbing was bush league, holdups of country stores, stealing from store tills and individual citizens indiscriminately. For instance, he and one Milo Creekmore stuck up a little country store in Lenapah, looking for a stockman's $700 that was supposed to be held there. They followed that with another store robbery, in which they robbed the clerk of some $500, magnanimously giving back to the fellow $10 of the $500 so that he might have something with which to do business.

Starr and his growing gang certainly were not getting rich. They were, however, beginning to create a reputation. Late in March of 1893, Starr and outlaw Frank Cheney struck the Caney Valley National Bank in Caney, Kansas, riding off with about $2,000. According to Starr he and Cheney had already "sacked the town of Choteau, just to keep in form, without any trouble at all." And then, on May 2, Starr and his embryo gang—six men in addition to Starr—stuck up a Katy train at Pryor Creek in Indian Territory, making off with some $5,000 in jewelry and money.

The gang members seem to have considered themselves professional criminals rather than warriors for the working day and lived high on the hog. They expended at least one hundred rounds of ammunition per day in practice, Starr boasted, and ate "every delicacy to be obtained."

In June of 1893 Starr followed up his success on the Katy with an ambitious attempt to rob a bank in Bentonville, Arkansas, but Starr was cautious at the start of this one as he had the gang's rifles brought into town in a hired buggy to escape attention. But once the robbery began, the citizenry of Bentonville quickly learned that their bank was being robbed. These stout people reached for their weapons, and Starr ran for his life amidst a torrent of gunfire. One of his men, Link Cumplin, was badly shot up, although he managed to stay on his horse and clear the town. Like other Starr accomplices Cumplin would finish the year dead from his wounds. One townsman took a round in the groin and another was wounded in the chin, but the gang was in full retreat, with a posse hot on their heels.

The gang would never ride together again. One, a morose man inevitably called "Happy Jack," was shot down two months later; a second was killed by lawmen in 1895. And Cheney had eaten his last meal, which was an officer's bullet to the head, in 1894.

As for Starr, he evaded the posse but was arrested not long afterward in Colorado Springs. After an ill-conceived jailbreak attempt, he faced a multitude of charges at Fort Smith. He was convicted of several robberies, and, to add insult to injury, the People's Bank of Bentonville sued Starr for $11,000 looted from the bank. Starr denied the claim, even though he was carrying much of the money when he was arrested.

But the big charge, the deadly one, was the murder of Wilson. That trial, too, ended in conviction, and Starr faced Judge Isaac Parker for sentencing. Judge Parker was famous for his stern lectures to condemned criminals, hanging sentences, and dwelling at length not only on the vileness of their earthly crimes but also on the imminent and daily danger posed to their immortal souls. The judge gave Starr a twenty-minute speech on morality and salvation and sentenced him to die.

That should have been the end of Henry Starr, but it wasn't. The US Supreme Court reversed the conviction, and the matter was remanded and set for a second trial. Meanwhile, Starr remained in the Fort Smith jail with as choice a collection of murderers and other worthless scum as any lockup has ever held.

Crawford Goldsby, the bloody-handed felon better known as Cherokee Bill, smuggled in a pistol. Nobody could get at Cherokee Bill, however, and he seemed to have plenty of ammunition. The standoff might have continued indefinitely, except for Henry Starr. Starr boldly walked into the cell where Cherokee Bill had taken refuge and talked him out of his weapon.

On retrial Starr was again convicted of the Wilson murder and again sentenced to death. And again the Supreme Court reversed. Judge Parker left the bench not long afterward and was replaced by Judge John Rogers. Judge Rogers entertained a plea of manslaughter, and Starr went off for a stiff prison term of thirteen years and eight months. Starr could behave well when he wanted to, and after his mother appeared before the Cherokee Council, that body appealed for clemency to President Theodore Roosevelt. In 1901, impressed with the story of Starr's cool intervention with Cherokee Bill, the president telegraphed Starr: "[W]ill you be good if I set you free?" Starr said he would, and so, by the beginning of 1903, Henry Starr was a free man.

Starr settled in Tulsa and married a schoolteacher, Miss Ollie Griffin. Starr was not without worries, however, for the Arkansas authorities had still not forgotten Bentonville; Starr was safe, however, for Oklahoma authorities refused to extradite him, relying on an attorney general's opinion that that action was unlawful as it affected a member of the Civilized Tribes. So Starr remained free and, for a time, apparently stayed away from the outlaw trail.

Eventually, the lure of the bank heist and easy money were too much for Starr. With Kid Wilson, an old criminal associate now on parole from New York, he struck a country bank in Tyro, Kansas. Things got so hot as a result that Starr and Wilson fled all the way to Colorado, where they robbed a tiny bank in Amity. Moving on to Arizona, Starr settled there under an alias. Traced by a letter he sent to Oklahoma, he was arrested in Arizona and returned to Colorado, where an unsympathetic court gave him seven to twenty-five years in the Cañon City penitentiary. In the fall of 1913, after his usual good behavior, Starr was paroled, on the one condition being that he not leave the state of Colorado.

And for a while he didn't. He opened a small restaurant, but that venture did not prosper, and in due course Starr abandoned the eatery and left Colorado, taking with him the comely wife of a local merchant. There followed a long string of robberies in Oklahoma, none of them big paydays. Rewards were posted—"dead or alive" this time—but Starr was hard to find, even though he was living in Tulsa. He even had the audacity to write the governor of Oklahoma, denying he had anything to do with any robberies, a profoundly unconvincing tactic reminiscent of Jesse James.

But Starr's luck was about to run out. In March of 1915 he decided to replenish his funds by raiding the bank in Stroud, a prosperous town about dead center in Oklahoma. He rode into town on horseback with six hoodlums to help him, a force that should have sufficed to cow the citizens of peaceful Stroud. And this gang should have been enough to accomplish the bank robber's ideal, the dream for which the Dalton Gang had gotten itself destroyed in Coffeyville twenty-three years before. They were going to rob two banks at once.

On March 27, 1915, at about 9:00 a.m., Starr and his crew rode into Stroud and set to work. At first the robbery went according to plan. Starr divided his force into two parties of three men, and they entered simultaneously the First National and the Stroud State Bank. Starr led the column that would raid the State Bank, brandishing a short rifle he had carried stuffed down his pants leg. As his partners covered two bankmen and a customer with pistols, Starr got $1,600 in loose cash, and then he demanded that bookkeeper J. B. Charles open the safe, or Starr would kill him.

"You'll have to kill me, then," said Charles coolly, "because I don't know the combination." Starr then threatened bank vice president Sam Patrick, who just as coolly told the outlaw leader that the safe had already been opened for the day's operating cash but was then reclosed and its time lock reset for the next day. Frustrated, Starr snatched Patrick's diamond stickpin and herded him, Charles, and a customer out into the street.

Over in the First National, Starr's companions found the safe open and swept up more than $4,000. When Starr joined them, they collected four bank employees and five customers to use as human shields. Herding these nine men in front of them, along with the hostages from the State Bank, the whole bandit gang walked deliberately toward their horses. But word of the holdup had spread through the town, and armed citizens were beginning to collect.

Their first shots were ineffective, and Starr's gang blazed away up and down the street to keep the townsmen at bay. Starr, hiding behind bankman Patrick, snapped a shot at Charley Guild, a shot that drove the shotgun-toting horse buyer quickly to cover behind a building.

More of Stroud's angry citizens were opening up on the outlaws. One in particular proved to be an especially deadly marksman. Seventeen-year-old Paul Curry had seen the robbery unfold from the yard of his parents' home nearby. Curry now ran into a butcher shop and came out with a sawed-off Winchester rifle. Taking cover behind some barrels in front of his father's grocery store, young Curry smashed Starr's leg with a round that tore into the outlaw's left thigh. When the bandit raised his weapon to return the fire, Curry yelled, "Throw away that gun or I'll kill you!" Convinced that this cool, tough youngster meant what he said, Starr dropped his weapon and fell back on the ground.

By this time the rest of the gang, abandoning their leader, had run to the stockyards, where they had tethered their all-important horses. They mounted up in haste and began to ride hard for safety, but bandit Lewis Estes was having trouble controlling his horse. Young Curry fired once more, and the bullet smashed into Estes's shoulder, breaking it and tearing into a lung. Waving a pistol, the outlaw forced two of the hostages to help him climb into the saddle, and all five bandits rode clear of the town.

Estes managed to stay on his horse for about a mile and half until he fainted from loss of blood and was pitched out of the saddle. His companions, as compassionate for him as they had been for Starr, took his horse and left him on the ground. Recovered by a posse, he was returned to town and taken to the office of Dr. John Evans, where Starr already lay. The bandit leader readily admitted to his identity and encouraged the close-mouthed Estes to do the same.

As the doctor dug the rifle bullet out of Starr's leg, Starr asked, "What did the kid shoot me with?" A hog rifle, somebody said, and Starr reacted with embarrassment. "I'll be damned. I don't mind getting shot, knew it had to happen sooner or later. But a kid with a hog gun—that hurts my pride."

Starr did have the good grace to congratulate Curry on his courageous stand. The young man told Starr he would use the reward money, $1,000, to get an education, and Starr is reported to have said, "You're all right, boy."

Meanwhile, a posse pursued the fleeing bandits, and the telephone—that new and handy crime-fighting tool—sent lawmen, volunteers, and even state militia chasing after the remains of the gang from all directions. Much of the pursuit was by automobile, and the pursuers came very close. But in the end they were foiled by the cross-country mobility of the mounted bandits and their own inability to quickly hire or borrow horses for the pursuit.

At the trial Starr entered a plea of guilty, to everybody's surprise, and then went off to prison in McAlester with a twenty-five-year sentence. Estes got five years. While in prison Starr went into his good behavior mode, and he was back on the street again in less than four years. His chief aide and support in this quick return to liberty was Kate Barnard, who was Oklahoma's first commissioner of "Charities and Corrections."

To her credit Kate was a holy terror to slothful or uncaring officials and did much good in improving conditions in state hospitals. She also cordially detested the penal system, which she considered medieval, and thought herself a perceptive judge of the character of those confined there. "I have studied men," she said, "until I know from the shape of their hands and head, the gait of their walk, and the contour of their faces, much of their mode of life and the character of their thoughts."

She was convinced that Starr would now walk the paths of virtue and thought he had made "one of the sincerest efforts at reformation of all the 20,000 convicts I have known." Maybe this redoubtable lady did have some powerful insight into the souls of felons, but in Starr's case she—and others, including the prison chaplain—had been thoroughly bamboozled.

Starr now settled in Tulsa and became involved in the burgeoning film industry. He bought an interest in a firm called the Pan-American Motion Picture Company, and with it produced a silent movie, *Debtor to the Law*. This film, an account of the Stroud debacle, used many of that town's citizens as actors, including young Curry, playing himself. *Debtor to the Law* was very successful, and a series of other films followed.

At that point in his life, after serving prison sentences in Colorado and Oklahoma, Starr had every chance to change his outlaw lifestyle. And for a while it seemed that he would do so. However, not even the bonds of matrimony—he was married twice—could wean Starr away from the excitement of being a professional criminal.

In spite of the fact that he had not had much luck robbing banks in Arkansas, Starr decided to hit yet another Arkansas town. This time he tried the People's National Bank in the little town of Harrison, not far from Bentonville.

On February 18, 1921, Starr and three other men drove into Harrison in a Nash automobile and entered the bank. None of them wore a mask, although Starr seems to have worn a pair of cheap glasses, perhaps as a rudimentary disguise. The outlaws had every expectation of a successful haul, for there was some $30,000 in the bank.

At first the holdup went just as planned. The robbers pushed up to the cashier's windows and covered bank president Marvin Wagley and cashier Cleve Coffman, pushing out of the way Ruth Wilson, a bookkeeper for a grocery firm who was in the midst of making a deposit for her boss.

"Hands up!" yelled the bandits. Then repeatedly warned Coffman to "keep quiet; don't move." One of them then went inside the working area of the bank while a second man began to herd everybody else toward the vault. Starr had thoughtfully brought along a pillow case, which he now opened. At gunpoint, he told Coffman to do what he was told. "You work with me and I'll work with you." By now the robbers had to watch not only Coffman, Wagley, and Ruth Wilson, but two other female employees and three more customers. Starr and his men also leveled their weapons at sixty-eight-year-old William J. Myers, who was a director and onetime president of the bank.

Myers had just entered his office at the rear of the bank, walking right into the middle of the robbery in progress. Having no other option, he dutifully raised his hands and followed one of the robber's orders by walking into the bank vault. But Myers apparently believed in prior planning, because he had long since arranged for a back door to the vault—what he called his "bandit trap"—specifically for just such an occasion. He had also secreted a loaded 1873 Winchester at the rear of the vault.

Starr finished sweeping the depositors' money into a sack, and he now ordered Coffman to open the safe. Coffman began to turn the dial, with the outlaw leader looking over his shoulder. When the door swung open Starr started to reach inside. At that moment Myers opened fire from inside the vault and Starr went down. "Don't shoot!" he is supposed to have yelled. "Don't shoot, don't shoot anybody. I am the one that is shot; don't shoot a man who is down."

Myers advanced out of the vault, his weapon trained on Starr. Oddly enough, the outlaw asked Myers to remove the cheap glasses he was wearing. Myers did so, then pressed on after Starr's companions, who had not stayed to fight or save their leader. They ran for it, in fact, tearing out of town in their automobile and leaving their boss behind. Myers ran outside and blazed away at the Nash as it raced off down the street, hitting one tire and blowing out the windshield.

Hastily organized citizens' posses pursued, but all they found was the Nash, abandoned and set on fire. In the days to come authorities would arrest three other men for complicity in the crime, but for now all eyes were on the desperately wounded Henry Starr. At first, Starr would not reveal who his cohorts were, and simply asked to see George Crump, once a

US Marshal. Crump was not in town, but his son was, and the younger man positively identified Starr.

So once again the celebrated king of the bank robbers was down and hurt and back in the hands of the law. Once more he had been shot down by an ordinary citizen who objected to Starr's larcenous ways, and this time the hurt would be permanent.

As he lay on a cot in a jail cell, Starr was visited by Coffman, the bank cashier, and on another occasion by an official of a bank in Seligman, Missouri, who identified Starr as one of the men who had robbed his bank the previous year, just before Christmas. Lawmen spent some time with him too, and at last Starr began to give them some information. He also told one physician, Dr. T. P. Fowler, that "I was in debt $20,000 and had to have money, so I turned bank robber again. I am sorry, but the deed is done."

Myers's bullet had lodged in the outlaw's spine, from which it was carefully removed by Dr. J. J. Johnson. The outlaw survived the operation, but the doctor opined that Starr's life was now chiefly in danger from blood poisoning. He also ran the risk of fatal uremic poisoning, the doctor said, because the slug had torn through one kidney on its way to the backbone.

The doctors did all they could for Henry Starr, but it soon became obvious to them, and to Starr, that he was finished. His present and ex-wife were both contacted, along with his mother and his son. Staring death in the face, Starr now began to lose some of his outlaw cockiness. "I am going to die," he said, "and I am anxious to make my peace with God." He also said he would give some useful information to the sheriff, which he did.

This time there would be no encore for the Bearcat. He lasted four days, slipped into a coma, and died.

A great many honest depositors and bank employees did not shed a single tear. They would not miss in the slightest a boastful professional criminal who lived off the sweat of other people. No amount of weeping and learned lamentation about society's evils would change the fact that Henry Starr was a career thug, a thug by choice, a thug who found it easier to steal what other people earned than work for himself.

Henry Starr was blessed by nature with considerable intelligence and an iron constitution, both of which assets he chose to squander in robbing other people, running from the law, and wasting his years sitting in prison. Boastful and arrogant, it is the real measure of the man that on the day before his death, sliding toward oblivion, he still bragged to his doctors that he had "robbed more banks than any man in America."

Where he was going, that dubious record would do him precious little good.

Curtains for the Verdigris Kid

Braggs was a bustling little settlement about nine miles east of Fort Gibson, not far from Muskogee. The settlement was named after Solomon Bragg, a white man who settled in the Illinois District of the Cherokee Nation and married a Cherokee woman. Bragg had built a gristmill in the area, something of an essential for a growing farm town. Later on, the Iron Mountain Railway pushed its line down the Arkansas Valley and called its local stop Bragg Station.

In 1886 Bragg Station, now called Braggs, got its own post office, set up in John Patrick's store. Tom Madden opened a second store, and the town grew to include, besides the gristmill, a doctor's office, a feed store, and a lumberyard. The little town also boasted a blacksmith's shop; a hotel; a small bank; a grocery; a one-room school; and the Methodist church, which was served from time to time by itinerant preachers.

Store owner Tom Madden, a Cherokee, had enemies to fear, so much so that he carried a gun in an innocuous paper bag. There had been, said the *Muskogee Phoenix*, "bad blood between Madden and certain other parties at Braggs for some time and that there would be bloodshed was not unexpected." The violence finally erupted in April of 1896, and Madden either didn't have his paper bag with him or he couldn't reach inside it in time. He was shot down in front of his store in the middle of the morning.

What happened to Madden was just one in a long line of murders and other violence that plagued this tiny town, making it the sort of place the Verdigris Kid would love. Sam McWilliams—the Verdigris Kid—had started his criminal career in a humble way, by stealing three cows from a settler. (McWilliams acquired his Verdigris Kid handle because his family lived along the Verdigris River.) He soon graduated to greater things, allying himself with the Cook Gang as they terrorized eastern Indian Territory. With the Cook outfit, he made himself a reputation of sorts in several robberies—of individuals, a bank, post office, stage, and train.

McWilliams was also part of a gunfight with a deputy marshal's posse out on the Caney River in northeastern Indian Territory, a fracas in which he took a bullet in the leg. He was treated by Dr. David Reece of Braggs.

Now it was March of 1895, and a band of outlaws came riding into Braggs. The old Cook Gang was no more, but Sam McWilliams hadn't learned a thing from the fate of his companions. On this day the gang included McWilliams, George Sanders, and Sam Butler, although there may have been others in the group as well. They headed for the store run by Tom Madden, herding ahead of them whatever male citizens they encountered. Along the way they stuck up and disarmed lawman Ed Barbee, who did not recognize the riders as outlaws until he was looking down their gun barrels.

Dismounting, McWilliams and Sanders pushed inside Madden's store where they helped themselves to whatever took their fancy. They would make a leisurely job of robbing the store and then rob the storekeeper when he arrived for the day's business. Butler posted himself out in front of the store to intercept anybody wanting to go inside.

There was no resistance by the townsmen. Nevertheless, at some time during the robbery, an unarmed man was shot down.

The *Edmond Sun-Democrat* reported somewhat obscurely that "the clerk, a young white man and son of the depot agent at Braggs, started to run out at the back door and were [sic] shot by the outlaws." This reference is almost surely to young Joe Morris, a clerk at Madden's, son of the railroad agent at Braggs.

However, as the pistol-waving Butler swaggered in the street and his comrades dallied inside the store, help for the town was on the way. Madden lived within sight of his store and was alarmed when, through his spyglass, he saw people standing on the store porch with their hands raised. With more courage than sense, he wanted to leave his house and fight, but his wife's cooler head prevailed. She insisted that he go after law officers, who lived about a mile away. Madden finally took her advice and used his horse instead of his gun. The officers he found were a pair of tough Cherokee deputy sheriffs, Johnson Manning and Hiram Stevens. These two lawmen hurried into town.

McWilliams and Sanders were in no hurry about robbing Madden's place, apparently fully enjoying playing the role of big-time outlaws. Not content with stealing whatever money Madden may have had in the till, they spent as long as forty minutes decorating themselves inside the store. "They removed their old shoes and put on new boots," said the *Weekly Elevator,* and "new clothes and a large number of silk handkerchiefs were selected. One of the bystanders was made to lead up a fine road [sic] horse that was hitched in the street, unsaddle one of the roan horses belonging to the robbers, and place the saddle on the roan."

The *Indian Journal* added dryly that the two outlaws "took things leisurely and picked out such goods as they wanted. Each had a suit apiece, and the two inside were picking out gloves when Butler warned them of the approach of Johnson Manning and Hiram Stevens."

Their posturing and preening abruptly ended, and McWilliams and Sanders ran to the door of Madden's store and opened fire on the lawmen, killing Manning's horse. Manning and Stevens returned fire, and their shooting was deadly. McWilliams went down for keeps, shot through the center of the chest. He was just nineteen.

Lawman Barbee, disarmed by the outlaws, ran through the line of fire between them and the deputy sheriffs to snatch up McWilliams's rifle and get into the fight. It was probably at this point that Madden's clerk, Joe Morris, courageously tried to help capture Sanders and Butler, maybe by running for the depot. He was shot through the body for his pains and fell, mortally wounded.

A monumental gunfight followed, as the surviving outlaws tried to hold off not only the deputies but also a growing number of townspeople, armed and angry. In addition to Manning and Stevens, the early shooting was done by a merchant named Craig and a citizen named Ellis Petit. At the start of the fight, the outlaws sheltered behind one of their horses, but Petit dropped the horse, leaving the bandits exposed to a heavy and burgeoning hail of lead.

G. W. Slater, a citizen who lived north of Braggs, had been pushing cattle that morning with a cowboy named Jim Green. Slater and Green had ridden into town to get something to eat and had settled themselves comfortably in the dining room of the town's little hotel just before the war started in the street outside.

Stray rounds from the beginning of the gun battle seriously discommoded the two diners, blasting the dishes from their table, and both men ran from the hotel. They sought out and quickly found someone who Slater thought was a deputy US marshal, although Slater called the lawman Hiram Stevens. Their meal destroyed, Slater and Green volunteered to help capture the outlaws, a task that would turn out to be somewhat easier said than done. As Slater told the story years later, in the twilight of his life:

> We went behind the hotel and took our places at the corner of the building. One of the gang started around the corner and we shot him and his horse. This started a real battle. Other citizens came to our assistance and after a thirty minute battle we had killed all but one. He was trying to get out of town and was shooting back toward us. I had no more ammunition, so I picked up a gun belonging to one of the gang. . . . Butler's gun fell from his hands and he rode away speedily.

"At the end of the battle," said this citizen much later, "there were thirteen dead men and twenty-seven dead horses. Those were very exciting days."

Exciting days indeed. But it would appear that the Braggs fight got even more exciting as it ripened with time in Slater's memory. In fact, there is no certainty that more than two criminals died in the shootout in front of Madden's store, although some other recollections by area pioneers do indeed suggest that the outlaw casualty list may have been much higher.

One early settler named Albert Barry much later recalled a report that "five of the outlaws had been killed." Earlier that day, Barry said, he had sold ammunition to two men in a store at a settlement called Illinois Station. Barry took a train to Braggs after hearing of the fight there, "to find the dead were lying on the station platform. The first two I saw were the men I had sold the ammunition to. . . . [T]he only one I personally knew was Sam McWilliams, known as the Verdigris Kid."

However many outlaws were really involved in the Braggs gunfight, there were too many tough lawmen and pugnacious citizens for the bandits to cope with. With McWilliams down, Sanders and Butler—with any other gang members who may have been along—fell back toward their horses, firing desperately at a growing host of enemies. Sanders didn't make it. Hit several times in the body and once in the temple, he went down for keeps in the dusty street of Braggs.

Butler managed to scramble to his horse through a hail of bullets and left Braggs at a high lope. Butler, according to the *Indian Journal*, was thought to be wounded; the *Weekly Elevator* asserted that he was hurt badly enough that he left a blood trail. Butler managed to elude pursuit, at least for the moment, but he did not have the sense either to put a lot of miles behind him in a hurry, or to stay away from his own familiar haunts.

The remains of Sanders and McWilliams were tossed in a wagon and hauled off to Eufaula, where Bill Cook, McWilliams's erstwhile leader, was languishing in jail. Officers brought the outlaw from his cell to view the corpses, and Cook, laying his hand affectionately upon the box where his former comrade lay, identified McWilliams. Thereafter the bodies were hauled off to Fort Smith and delivered to US Marshal George J. Crump. McWilliams's remains were worth $250; Sanders's were worth nothing.

With McWilliams and Sanders done, only the verminous Butler was at large. Once he got clear of the town of Braggs, he simply rode on home, leaving a reasonably clear trail behind him. On the night of August 1, 1895, Deputy Marshal John Davis followed Butler's track to what was then called the Henry Chambers place, up on the Verdigris River. There lived both Butler's wife and his mother, and there, sure enough, was Butler also.

When Butler saw Davis approaching, he jumped to his feet, grabbed his gun, and fired, driving a bullet through the lawman's right side. Davis fell from his horse, mortally wounded, but his return fire smashed into Butler's chest and killed him instantly. Marshal Davis lived only about an hour after the fight, but at least he had the satisfaction of leaving the world a cleaner place.

Old Tom Starr
Implacable

In the fall of 1843, Tom Starr, two of his brothers, and Arch Sanders raided the house of a Cherokee political rival. Not content with murdering only the rival, the Starrs also killed his wife and a traveler staying the night at his house. Worst of all, after the brothers set fire to his house, a child ran out of the flames. A Cherokee acquaintance of Tom Starr's later passed along the story as Tom told it to him: "[A] little boy about five years old came running out and begged him not to kill him, and Tom . . . just picked him up and threw him in the fire. He said he didn't think God would ever forgive him for that and I said I didn't think He would either."

If Tom Starr didn't already have a reputation as a holy terror, he surely did after murdering the pleading child. With a price of $1,000 on each of their heads, Tom and his brothers ran for cover across the Arkansas, but they were far from through. Over time he, his brothers, and their followers are thought to have killed at least twenty men. And Tom himself said it was a good many more.

Old Tom was a formidable figure, intimidating just to look at. He was big, six foot five, and a powerful man. He wore his black hair down his shoulders, generally had his eyelashes plucked, and often sported a rawhide necklace, tastefully hung with the earlobes of men he had killed. He was remorseless and unforgiving, tough and grim, and a

terrible enemy, but he was born of a violent time in Cherokee country, when deep-seated loyalty was perhaps the most
valued quality in a man next to courage. Old Tom had more
than his share of both.

Back in 1836 and 1837, a number of Cherokee families traveled west from their ancestral homelands in Georgia, preferring
to move in their own time and at their own pace rather than
be driven west by US troops. Those who did not leave their
homes then would later be herded along what became known
as "the Trail of Tears." After the Removal Treaty had been
signed in 1835, only one question remained: When would the
Cherokee Nation move to the new lands to the west?

In 1833 the Starr clan, led by Tom's father, James, was
among the early immigrants to Indian Territory. A larger
group of eastern Cherokees arrived in the territory in 1838,
and the tribe split into two groups. One was the treaty party:
the signers of the treaty and their supporters. The others, led
by principal chief John Ross, formed a larger group, forcibly
removed from their ancestral lands by the US government.
Because they had vehemently objected to the voluntary relinquishment of those lands, they were known generally as the
antitreaty party. For a while there were actually two governments, and a great deal of bad blood between the two groups.

The old chief, John Ross, proposed a constitution that
would unify all the settlers under a single government. Those
who had settled in the territory earlier replied that "the newcomers in coming into a territory which already had an organized government accepted that government; and accordingly,
since the Western Cherokees had received and welcomed
their brother emigrants, the two people were already united."

The bitterness was a recipe for trouble, and in 1839 the anti-treaty faction's anger boiled over. A group of Cherokees hostile to the treaty men met in secret. To them assassination seemed to be the simple solution to their hatred for the men who had signed the detested treaty. So antitreaty militants murdered leaders of the faction that had signed away the old lands. They even dragged one from his sickbed, slashing the fingers of his wife when she tried to protect her husband.

In another case killers approached and asked their victim for medicine for a sick friend. He started toward his house to get it, and the reward for his kindness was a tomahawk buried in his face, followed by more hacking and chopping and several bullets pumped into his body.

The assassins also planned to kill James Starr, but he was warned in time to escape. He found temporary protection at Fort Gibson. He would shelter there several times, in later days, as violence became epidemic in the Goingsnake District of eastern Indian Territory.

Tom Starr and three more of James's sons, Bean, Washington, and Ellis, were the heart of the family. Along with a cousin, Suel Rider, the brothers went on the attack. The last straw for the Starrs came when some thirty of the Ross opposition struck the Starr homestead and shot down James Starr as he washed his face before breakfast.

They then murdered his crippled fourteen-year-old son, Buck, and would have killed three younger boys except that their mother and grandmother wrapped their arms around them. An early resident of the area, a doctor, later said that James Starr's wife faced the murderers and calmly told them that when Tom heard of the murders of her husband and son that he would settle with them.

Unwilling to kill the Starr women, the raiders then moved down the road and shot down Suel Rider in his own front yard. One of the Ross men then dismounted and stabbed Rider in the heart. They next attacked Washington Starr on the road. He was very badly injured, but he still managed to find cover and escape. As the killers were busy trying to do away with Washington Starr, one of James's young sons, Creek Starr, ran to Tom Starr's house, some two miles away, with news of the murders.

Victory had gone—temporarily—to the antitreaty men: When James Starr was buried, only the women of the family could safely attend the funeral. But the killers had missed Tom Starr, which would prove to be a fatal mistake, because Tom would never forget the injury to his family. A month or so later, Tom told his wife, Catharine, "I will get every man who killed Buck and Pa. I will not stop killing until I do, and I will never be taken alive."

When Tom Starr said something, he generally meant every word of it, and he and his surviving brothers got to work quickly. Stan, the Cherokee who had stabbed the wounded Suel Rider as he lay on the ground, was soon a corpse himself. Tom Starr and a band of supporters sent Wheeler Fought into a local Indian dance where Stan was enjoying himself. The plan was to have Fought fill Stan with booze and later tell him that a jug of whiskey was hidden in a fallen tree.

The tactic worked, for later in the evening, a drunken Stan thought of the jug and rode his horse toward the tree. As he did, Starr's band shot him out of the saddle and then stabbed him to death, just as he had killed Suel Rider. Fought's loyalty to the treaty party cost him his own life. Once the antitreaty party found out that he had lured Stan to his death, Fought was also killed.

Tom not only shed the blood of his enemies but also delighted in ravaging their property. He was fond of stealing the opposition's slaves and selling them farther to the south, and he coveted their livestock, too. Not long after Tom's first murders, the Starr brothers were jumped by a posse of Indian police while driving stolen mules and horses toward the Texas line. Bean Starr was killed in the ensuing fight, and later Starr cohort Charles Smith—himself the son of a murdered treaty signer—fatally stabbed a lieutenant in the Indian police unit that had killed Bean. Smith did not last long himself, hunted down by the police and killed while resisting arrest.

The violence continued. Early in 1845 another signer of the treaty was also murdered, and the son of an ex-chief was killed during a council at Fort Gibson. An April 1846 letter to Stand Watie, later a Confederate brigadier, gives some of the flavor of the times:

> You will doubtless recollect that . . . the murderer of
> James Starr was killed and scalped and that Fought was
> caught for decoying him and has since been hung. Since
> that time Oto Cornsilk has been killed. . . . Barrow Justice
> has been caught, tried and was hung yesterday. . . . John
> Brown & his company caught a horse thief and they
> killed him . . . rumored that he and his company . . .
> have cut up another man . . . in his own house. I forgot to
> mention that another man was killed at Ellis Harlan's . . .
> I think there is now to be no end to bloodshed, since the
> Starr boys & the Riders have commenced revenging the
> death of their relatives. . . . Murders in the county have
> been so frequent until the people care little about hearing
> these things.

In November of 1845 a group of disguised riders burned down the home of Return Meigs, the chief's son-in-law. Two

Cherokees who had seen the arsonists were murdered, but Meigs said the raiders were the three surviving Starr boys and Ellis West. Within days more violence erupted, leaving eleven men dead and another eighteen wounded. More bloodshed followed, and the US Army sent dragoons into Cherokee country to restore some semblance of order. More killings followed, however, and more members of the treaty party fled into Arkansas.

The burning of Meigs's house and the murder of the two witnesses to the arson were the last straw for the antitreaty contingent. In 1846 President James Polk at last stepped in to deal with the simmering mess in the Cherokee country. By now there were no less than three separate groups vying for power. Polk suggested that perhaps the Cherokee country should be split into three separate political entities, and a bill to that end appeared in the House.

Nobody liked his radical suggestion and the Cherokees uneasily became one nation. Part of the accord was a general pardon for all Cherokees for all offenses and crimes, a provision especially valuable for the Starr clan.

Tom Starr moved into the rugged southwestern corner of the Canadian District near Briartown—now in Muskogee County—in the great bend of the South Canadian River. When the Civil War broke out, he went off to war as a scout for Stand Watie's Confederate brigade, in opposition to tribal Union supporters, called "pin Indians" (from their custom of wearing crossed pins on their shirts as a symbol of support for the Union). At least a couple of accounts assert that Tom Starr "fought alongside" and was visited by the odious Missouri bushwhacker Quantrill, although this seems, at best, a very remote possibility.

The war did little to ease the old hatreds that split the Cherokee Nation. Stand Watie, as a Confederate brigadier, wrote his wife in the autumn of 1863, commenting casually on more killing, and on the burning of the opposition chief's home. "Killed a few pins in Tahlequah," he wrote. "They had been holding council. I had the old Council House set on fire and burned down."

After the war Tom went back to his civilian enterprises. According to legend, his business consisted mostly of whiskey running—forbidden by federal law in the Indian nations—and trafficking stolen cattle and horses. He also operated the first ferry on the South Canadian River.

By now he presided over a small army of kinfolk: his eight sons and two daughters and all their offspring. Old Tom's empire also included an extensive collection of in-laws: Even if lawmen had tried to ride into Starr country to arrest Tom, they would have needed a battalion to smoke him out.

Starr's home was a friendly place for ex-bushwhackers, including the Younger boys and, it is said, the James brothers. Such men, moving fast and keeping to the brush, could always find a meal and safety with Tom Starr. It was during this postwar period that the Starr empire got its name of "Younger's Bend."

Stories about Old Tom were legion. One tells of a $500 bet on a horse race between Starr and a transient gambler. Seeing Starr was not carrying a gun, the gambler, with more hubris than good sense, made the mistake of threatening Starr, saying no matter which horse won, he would just take the money. Understandably, that irritated Starr, and he told the gambler so.

It is hard to imagine a professional betting man being that stupid, especially if he knew Tom's reputation. Still, according to legend, when Tom's horse won, the gambler reached for his gun. Old Tom grabbed his bowie knife and threw it so hard that it pierced the gambler's body and stuck in the ground.

Other tales of Tom Starr are somewhat less grim. There's the story of how he outwitted and unhorsed an entire company of soldiers who had been sent to capture him. Cutting down a section of telegraph wire, he stretched it across the road about waist high and led his pursuers into it. While the soldiers picked themselves up and recovered their horses, Tom Starr went his way chuckling. This tale is about as likely as the Easter Bunny, but it's typical of the mythology that inevitably grew up around any larger-than-life figure . . . and Tom Starr surely was that.

Whatever other illicit doings old Tom may have been up to, late in life he seemed to favor booze running as his preferred source of pocket change. For a while all went well, but in time his luck ran out. In June 1884 he was charged under federal law with running five gallons of whiskey into Cherokee country, and in December 1885 he was arrested on a warrant for selling four gallons more. Then in 1886 he was caught smuggling another gallon into Indian Territory and jailed at Fort Smith in lieu of a $300 bond.

When the Fort Smith grand jury met, it indicted him on the 1885 and 1886 offenses, and in November 1886 Tom appeared before Judge Isaac Parker of the Western District of Arkansas. Tom made the decision to plead guilty, probably not a wise idea, and Judge Parker gave him a year in prison on the first count and a consecutive six-month sentence on the second one. By the end of November, Tom was behind bars in the federal prison at Menard, Illinois. He would languish at Menard until early in 1888.

Maybe prison took something out of Tom Starr's free spirit. Maybe he had just been too long on the back roads of violence and anger to be happy on the placid paths of peace. In any case he did survive his erstwhile daughter-in-law, Belle, murdered from ambush near her Younger's Bend home in 1889.

Back from prison, Tom lived on at Younger's Bend in failing health, until he died in 1890. He was gone, but he would not be forgotten.

Elmer McCurdy Finds a Job He Can Do

A Second Career

Every once in a while, an outlaw comes along who lacks the minimal brainpower required to run with even the dumbest of gunslingers. One of these, the prince of dummies, was Elmer McCurdy. Elmer was a small-time crook, but he deserves a place in this book because of the bizarre manner in which he departed this life, and his subsequent adventures. Elmer wasn't content to stay buried in an outlaw's grave. Instead, he embarked on a second career after his death: He became a professional dummy.

Born in Maine, he drifted west around the turn of the twentieth century, worked at various ordinary jobs, and served a stint in the army. But at heart Elmer was without redeeming social value: a killer, a drifter, a jailbird, a thug with a string of aliases who decided he preferred train robbing to honest work.

In the spring of 1911, Elmer and another thug named Walter Jared and some other kindred spirits held up a train just north of the Oklahoma state line. This successful raid on the Missouri-Pacific was enough to entice Elmer into the holdup business. He and Jared recruited Jared's brother and laid plans for a holdup of the Missouri-Kansas-Texas (Katy) line.

In the first place Elmer's intelligence was faulty. He hadn't made sure that he was stalking the right train. He apparently

105

Elmer McCurdy, alias Frank Curtis, alias Frank
Davidson, killed near Pawhuska, Okla, Oct. 7, 1911

Elmer McCurdy, professional dummy *Western History Collections, University of Oklahoma Libraries*

wasn't worried about taking on the formidable deputies of Osage County either. These men had chased real outlaws, Daltons and such, and they knew how to deal with varmints who held up trains. Elmer hadn't yet started his raid, and he was already well out of his league.

On October 6, 1911, Elmer and his little gang of hoodlums stopped Katy train number 29 at night near Okesa, a little village in northeast Oklahoma. The gang uncoupled the engine and the express car from the rest of the train and moved them on down the line. Now it was time to reap the coveted bonanza they had waited for.

Forty-six dollars was all they found. Elmer had stopped the wrong train. Mean-spirited as well as stupid, Elmer stole the conductor's watch and two demijohns of whiskey and departed on foot, alone, into the Osage Hills, for years a popular safe haven for men on the run from the law. Elmer, sadly for his future, was neither Dalton nor Doolin, and the thickets and ravines of the Osage were no help to him. In addition to being terminally stupid, he was apparently no good at covering his tracks. Moreover, he grew drunker and drunker as he went, steadily working on the whiskey he had liberated from the train.

A posse with bloodhounds quickly picked up his trail, finding one of the demijohns, empty, along the way. That probably told them they weren't dealing with the smartest hen in the coop, and they pressed on. After a two-day chase, the pursuers ran Elmer to earth at the Revard farm out on the Big Caney River.

Elmer arrived at Revard's already well lubricated. He made matters worse by drinking for a while with some ranch hands before he finally headed for the barn to seek solace in sleep. He hadn't been snoring long before three Osage deputies appeared. Bob and Stringer Fenton and Dick Wallace, intelligent men, wisely considered it was downright unhealthy to go poking into a dark barn after an armed outlaw, however drunk he might be. And so they waited for the morning. Just after sunrise Elmer revived enough to look outside and was shocked to see three badges waiting for him.

At that, he made the last of his many mistakes: He decided to fight.

Short on brains, Elmer was long on courage. A more intelligent thief probably would have surrendered; he hadn't killed anybody during his botched holdup and so wasn't in danger of the rope. But Elmer elected to fight. "He took a shot at me first," said Bob Fenton. "Then he took a shot at Stringer. After that, he took three shots at Wallace before we opened fire."

Elmer traded shots with the posse for an hour or so until at last a lawman's bullet hit Elmer square and ventilated him permanently. The slug tore through the right side of Elmer's chest and bored on through his body, all the way into the lower abdomen, killing him.

That should have been the end of the line for Elmer. After all, he was a pip-squeak in the hierarchy of Oklahoma outlaws. When the smoke blew away at Revard's, the posse hauled Elmer's earthly remains off to Pawhuska, where Elmer was identified and handed over to the ministrations of Johnson's local undertaking emporium. Sensing a small windfall in a town where not very much exciting happened, the mortician preserved Elmer with an arsenic compound that ossified him, apparently transforming him into a sort of unwrapped mummy. He then stored Elmer in the back room of the undertaking parlor and charged the general public a nickel to look at him.

Elmer wasn't a big-time attraction, but a five-cent outlaw was better than no outlaw at all. Elmer was featured as "The Bandit Who Wouldn't Give Up," and he hung around Pawhuska until around 1916. But Elmer was about due for a career change, and his chance came when a tearful visitor approached the undertaker and announced that Elmer was his long-lost brother. The stranger pleaded, saying that he wanted to give him a decent burial in the family plot. The undertaker, a decent sort, took compassion on the visitor and handed what was left of Elmer over to his self-proclaimed kin. Not until too late did he learn that the man who took him was no relation at all: The man ran a carnival, and Elmer was off to new adventures.

Elmer apparently wasn't much of a star outside Pawhuska, at least not on the road. For a while he sat around in movie theater lobbies, as a come-on for a variety of Western films, and then he spent a couple of decades in storage, between jobs.

As the years went by, Elmer passed from hand to hand, traveling for a while with Sonney's Museum of Crime, a sort of mobile waxworks. In time Elmer moved on to Craft's Carnival Circus, finally ending up in something named the Hollywood Wax Museum in a place called the Nu-Pike Amusement Park. By this time covered with wax and distinctly aging, Elmer was featured as "The One-Thousand-Year-Old Man"—at least until the Hollywood Wax Museum went out of business.

Elmer had one more opportunity left, an outside chance at making the real big time. He had a chance now to appear in the Mount Rushmore Haunted House, but he lost out in his audition when it developed he had grown stiff as a plank with the years. Mount Rushmore turned poor Elmer down. Nobody in the museum business wanted a dummy who actually looked like one.

Perhaps in lieu of back rent, Elmer ended up the property of the owner of the Nu-Pike park. For some reason, that worthy painted Elmer with a concoction that glowed orange and red under ultra-violet light and fixed him up with a hangman's noose in an exhibit called *Laugh in the Dark Fun House*. Elmer's new boss thought Elmer was only a tired hunk of man-shaped papier-mâché: He didn't have the vision to recognize a star waiting to be born.

Elmer's great moment was still ahead of him, however, and it came through television. On December 8, 1976, the Fun House was the site of a truly exciting happening, the filming of an episode of *The Six Million Dollar Man*. Setting up for a camera shot, a technician asked a crew member to move what appeared to be a dummy, dangling forlornly in a noose from an overhead two-by-four.

As the dummy was moved, an arm fell off, and the horrified technicians found they had partially disassembled a real human being. What they thought was a battered dummy, an artificial human figure, wasn't artificial at all. It was real: petrified, certainly; much the worse for wear, to be sure; but apparently human. It was indeed human. It was Elmer.

The authorities were duly summoned and began the tedious business of identifying the desiccated remains. The Los Angeles County coroner, Dr. Thomas Noguchi, was no stranger to high-profile cases: His office had run a number of autopsies on the Hollywood rich and notorious. Still, this dummy, John Doe number 255, looked like a different kind of case altogether. Nameless unwrapped mummies didn't show up every day, even in Los Angeles. They are especially unusual when they appear in the middle of shooting a popular television show.

The coroner's investigators had their work cut out for them, starting with the difficulty they found in filling out the medical report. The search for Elmer's identity was not as hopeless as it first appeared. Incisions in what was left of Elmer told the examiner that Elmer had been professionally embalmed. He was full of arsenic, too, a practice embalmers had generally ceased about 1920. That gave the investigators a broad but workable window in time.

Then there was the cause of death, which provided more help to the searchers. While the slug that killed Elmer did not turn up inside the cadaver, its copper jacket did, and it was enough to identify the caliber of the round as .32-20. That gave the investigators something more to go on, for manufacture of the .32-20 ceased before the Second World War. The particular configuration of the bullet had first appeared on American ammunition about 1905.

So, between the copper jacket and the arsenic embalming, the investigators had narrowed the time of Elmer's death to a window of about fifteen years.

And then there was the other evidence. An alert coroner's examiner noted that Elmer's mouth contained items not usually found in such places, notably a 1924 penny and some ticket stubs, one of which bore the legend, "Louis Sonney's Museum of Crime, So. Main St., L.A." The coroner's examiners now began to trace Elmer's travels, working backward across the years.

The last owner of Elmer, Ed Liersch, said he'd gotten Elmer from a Mr. Singh at the Hollywood Wax Museum. Dave Friedman, described as a Hollywood filmmaker, told the press the Sonney outfit owned Elmer until it sold him to the Hollywood Wax Museum in 1968. Elmer had been dusted off in 1964, put back into service, and reexhibited. He even appeared in a 1967 Friedman epic called *She Freaks*. It is not recorded whether Elmer had a speaking part.

Louis Sonney, whose ticket stub ended up in Elmer's mouth, was a story all by himself. In 1921, according to one newspaper account, Sonney was a peace officer in Centralia, Washington, and there he managed the single-handed capture of Roy Gardner, a thoroughly rotten robber. Capitalizing on his well-earned reputation, and using a welcome $5,000 reward, Sonney went on the road with his own show, "The March of Crime."

Louis Sonney had been dead since 1949, but his son told investigators that his father had bought Elmer forty or fifty years before, showing him in the museum under his real name. After Louis Sonney's death, however, Elmer was stored in a Los Angeles warehouse with other attractions. There he languished until he was acquired by Mr. Singh, twenty-two years later.

111

There remained only the last piece in the puzzle to fit in place. That part was supplied by Dwayne Esper, an elderly resident of Phoenix. Esper said he'd gotten Elmer in about 1926 from a retired coroner in Tulsa. Esper was aware of Elmer's history, too, at least enough to state that he was an outlaw, shot in the early 1900s in a small town near Tulsa.

Probably without realizing it, the investigator added his own small spot of macabre comedy to the McCurdy saga: "The cadaver had supposedly robbed a bank in a small town near Tulsa, Oklahoma, and had been shot doing so."

The final confirmation of Elmer's identify was provided by Dr. Clyde Snow, world-famous forensic anthropologist, who flew to the West Coast from Oklahoma to examine Elmer and review the evidence. Dr. Snow found a scar on the cadaver's wrist, in a spot where Elmer was known to have a similar scar. Then the doctor went to a high-tech system of his own devising, never before used in Los Angeles County.

Dr. Snow used a pair of video cameras, linked to a special effects generator and wired to a monitor. One camera was focused on the mummy, showing him in profile. The other was aimed at a 1911 postmortem photograph of Elmer, also in profile, obtained from the University of Oklahoma Western History Collection.

The two profiles, projected simultaneously, turned out to match very closely. They were "remarkably coincident" in the doctor's words. The profile match wasn't conclusive, but it was powerfully bolstered by the considerable accumulation of other hard evidence.

On the basis of all the evidence, Dr. Snow concluded that the cadaver was indeed Elmer beyond reasonable doubt, and

Dr. Noguchi signed a death certificate to that effect. All of this fuss had made Elmer something of a celebrity. There is even a tale that Elmer appeared on a national evening news program, without, of course, speaking.

Elmer returned to Oklahoma at last in April of 1977. He arrived as the guest of the Oklahoma Historical Society and the Indian Territory Posse of Westerners, a body of public-spirited Oklahomans who aim to preserve the state's considerable historical heritage.

Elmer had a fine funeral, even in a spring rain, drawn to his last rest in an antique horse-drawn hearse, the kind with elaborate draped curtains and glass windows in the sides so you can catch a last glimpse of the departed. He even got a mounted escort from the posse and a tasteful graveside eulogy.

So Elmer's long odyssey was over at last. Now he awaits the Last Trumpet north of Oklahoma City in the cemetery at Guthrie, once the state capital. He lies there under a decent memorial and also under a couple of cubic yards of concrete, thoughtfully provided to discourage the morbid from disturbing Elmer's rest.

He sleeps not far from real outlaw Bill Doolin, which no doubt would have pleased Elmer. He is surrounded by an assortment of pioneers, outlaws, and politicians, which perhaps suggested this bit of doggerel, the last word on Elmer McCurdy:

> *Rest in peace, dear Elmer,*
> *Beneath this Okie sky,*
> *Where many an outlaw slumbers,*
> *And politicians lie.*

Belle Starr
Heap Big Smoke and No Fire

Oklahoma's most famous female outlaw was something of a fraud, a minor player who ended up a star courtesy of the *Police Gazette* and a series of sensational books. Nobody knows today what crimes Belle Starr actually committed beyond minor horse theft, but the mass of legends about her qualifies her for a place in the pantheon of Oklahoma criminals.

Her long shadow does loom over at least one brutal offense: Belle is said to have accompanied her husband, Jim Reed, on the especially ugly robbery of a wealthy Oklahoma Indian up in the Choctaw Nation of a purported $30,000. The victim, Watt Grayson, at first refused to tell Reed and two other bandits where he kept his cash. They then threw a noose around his neck and hoisted him clear of the ground until he nearly strangled.

This cruelty having no result, his tormentors turned on Grayson's wife and began using the same torture. At this Grayson had enough, and the bandits got their money.

Belle had traveled a long road to Indian Territory. She was a Missouri girl, born plain old Myra Maybelle Shirley on a farm near Carthage, Missouri. Her father was a successful man, but the horrors of the Civil War cast their ugly shadow across the land and the family's world changed. They were living in Carthage then, and Myra Maybelle got an education at the Carthage Female Academy. The stories about her tell that she

Belle Starr, showing off as usual
Western History Collections, University of Oklahoma Libraries

received an excellent education for the time and also became an accomplished musician.

Her father was still prospering, now in the inn-keeping business, but the Civil War largely ruined him. His eldest son, Bud, joined the pro-Confederacy bushwhackers and was killed, and in time the town of Carthage was burned. There are all sorts of stories about young Belle's heroics during the war, "her hot Southern blood," as one sensational writer put it, "fired to deeds of valor." Legend has Belle galloping about the countryside carrying messages for her brother's guerrilla band or acting as a spy.

She was "frequently with Cole Younger and the James boys," the story goes, even though they rode with different guerrilla units.

With Bud's death and the loss of much of his property, the senior Shirley had enough of the vicious border war and moved his family south, settling near Scyene, Texas, now a part of Dallas. There, in 1866, Belle married a hoodlum called Jim Reed, already on the run from the law. Two years later a daughter appeared and was named Rosie; Belle called her "her pearl," however, and she remained Pearl for the rest of her days. Pearl would grow up to be both prostitute and madam, but that was a long way in the future.

The Reeds lived for a time in the sanctuary of Old Tom Starr's spread down on the Canadian River in Indian Territory, but in 1871 they were living in California, where their son, Ed, was born. Reed was a professional criminal, and by now he was charged with murder. There are tales that Belle was his confederate, at least to the point of fencing horses her husband had stolen. The legends about her robbing and murdering—which have no solid foundation—are probably no more than a part of the mythology surrounding Belle's life.

Besides the torture of Watt Grayson, one 1874 incident is probably the best known: the robbery of the San Antonio–Austin stagecoach. There is no real evidence that Belle had anything to do with the crime, let alone that she was part of the holdup itself, but Reed certainly did. He lasted until the summer of 1874, when he came in second in a gunfight with a deputy in Paris, Texas. There is a charming tale that Belle refused to identify what was left of Reed to deny the officer the reward. Nice story, but again without foundation. Belle was now a widow, but she would not remain one.

She is said to have dallied with Bruce Younger up in southern Kansas, maybe even marrying him, but whatever the relationship was, it did not last. And then, in the summer of 1880, she married Sam Starr down in the Cherokee Nation. Sam was the son of Old Tom Starr, one of the really ferocious fighting men of the territory, and the couple settled on Old Tom's property. Somewhere along the way the place began to be called Younger's Bend, which spawned still another legend: that Belle named the place, still carrying a torch for Cole Younger, the father of her Pearl. This seems to be no more than still another folk myth, for the place was named by Old Tom, who apparently admired the Missouri outlaw. To his dying day Cole denied that Pearl was his, and in this he was probably telling the truth for a change.

In 1883 Belle and her new husband did a short stretch at the Detroit House of Corrections for horse stealing, but when their time was up, they returned to Younger's Bend. In 1876 Sam Starr was attending a dance when he ran into a hated adversary, Frank West. The two wasted no time in reaching for their guns, and in a few minutes both men were dead. Belle was once more a widow.

Here the mists of mythology settle over the scene again. Belle was not through playing around with disreputable outlaw types, although it's not entirely clear who her lovers might have been. She is quoted as having said, "I am a friend to any brave and gallant outlaw." She was more than a friend to a whole passel of outlaws, if legend is anywhere near accurate. A host of stories have her cavorting with a veritable galaxy of luminaries in the outlaw world, including—at least—Jack Spaniard, Jim French, Jim July (who ended up answering to the handle of Jim

Starr), and a man much younger than the now-aging Belle, one Blue Duck.

Whatever carnal delights Belle may have indulged in, she also paid attention to her home at Younger's Bend. And that was probably what ended her life prematurely. For she had at least one sharecropper tenant, a man called Ed Watson. He had come out of Arkansas but was originally from Florida, where he was wanted for murder, among other things. Belle apparently found out about Ed's nasty past . . . and it was a little too much knowledge.

The two got into a dispute when Belle, afraid of more trouble with the authorities if she were discovered harboring a fugitive, told Watson to leave her land and sent him a letter returning his rent money. The two argued, and Belle incautiously told the man that while federal marshals might not be interested in him, "the Florida officers might."

Although others were suspected then and afterward—including her own son—it seems pretty clear that a furious Watson determined to close Belle's mouth forever. Either he or somebody else waylaid her and blew her out of the saddle with a shotgun. And so, in February of 1889, Belle passed to her reward, whatever that might be. She was buried at Younger's Bend, according to a legend with a revolver in her hand. The myth was off to a good start.

Watson was charged but never tried. There simply was not enough evidence to take to court. But knowing that Jim July Starr would almost certainly try to kill him, Watson left the state and at last ended up back in Florida, where he went on killing, running up a tally of as many as twelve people. In time he ran afoul of some tough peace officers who filled him full of holes.

As for Pearl, she carried on with her prostitute's career. Finally exiled from Fort Smith after repeated arrests, she drifted west, dying in an Arizona hotel in the summer of 1925.

In December of 1896 Belle's son, Ed Reed, got full of tarantula juice in a saloon run by a man named Tom Clark. Reed got rowdy, "brandishing his six shooter in a very careless way and abusing the bystanders and shooting up the place generally" as the *Muskogee Phoenix* put it. Clark was understandably upset, and some hard words passed between the men. Reed left but came back with a Winchester and threatened Clark. It turned out to be a bad idea, because Clark was quicker and shot Reed twice, whereof he expired.

It was as well that Belle was not around to see the end of her children.

The Buck Gang
Evil Incarnate

Mrs. Henry Hassan pleaded, but it didn't do her any good. Lewis Davis forced Mrs. Hassan to leave her house and go to the barn, where he raped her. When she tried to appeal to him, he threatened to kill her husband and throw her small children in the creek. When Davis was finished, the whole Buck Gang joined in.

Their lust satisfied, the gang turned on Hassan, whom they forced to ride with them to a field some two miles away. There they forced him to jump into a pool of water. One account says they knew Hassan had been a professional buck-and-wing dancer and so they made him dance, shooting at his heels to liven up their antics. During this merriment up came an unsuspecting neighbor of the Hassans, Dick Ryan. He and Hassan were forced to fight each other for the gang's amusement.

When they had finally had all the amusement they could stand, they rode away, threatening that if the two men ever testified against the gang, friends of the gang would kill Hassan and Ryan.

And so the gang's brutal career was well launched, and more was to come. The Buck Gang didn't have a long run as outlaw careers went, but while they were at it, they instilled fear and disgust in the people of Indian Territory unmatched by any other gaggle of criminals. What made the Buck Gang especially loathsome was that they were fond of committing

Quintessential evil: the Buck Gang *Western History Collections, University of Oklahoma Libraries*

the ultimate sin of the time: They were rapists. While murder and robbery and larceny were all common offenses, rape was considered especially heinous, so much so that it carried the death penalty in Judge Parker's much-feared court at Fort Smith. The Bucks indulged in some larceny, but they didn't seem especially interested in robbing trains or banks or stores. They simply brutalized people.

Had any of the real outlaws of Indian Territory been interviewed, they too would have had nothing good to say about the Buck Gang. Despite their brutality the Bucks never made it big, and they hadn't really started big either.

Instead Rufus Buck had started small. He had a string of minor crimes behind him, he had done time in the pokey at Fort Smith, and now he thought he was headed for the big time.

He is said to have bragged about how he would lead a gang that would eclipse the criminal record of every other outlaw in the territory. In the end, however, he managed just thirteen days of lawlessness, a short career, but ugly enough as long as it lasted.

He led a band of young men as depraved as he was. He started with Lewis Davis and Luckey Davis. Later he would add Sam Sampson and Maoma July. Like Buck all of them had criminal records and had spent some time in the Fort Smith jail. All five proved to be unusually vicious, even for those violent times.

Buck was the son of a prominent Euchee Indian politician, who either wouldn't or couldn't control his hoodlum son. Buck's father was a staunch advocate of Indian independence, and his son chose that theme to justify his crime wave. After one particularly vicious rape, he piously announced that in the future whites would think ten times before they took Indian land. Maybe Buck felt a need to justify his crimes in the holy cause of Indian independence. In any event his ugly offenses angered the Indian population as much as they did the white. Within days he would have the Lighthorse (the Indian police) on his back trail as well as federal officers and angry citizens.

The violence began when the gang rustled twenty-three hogs and managed to sell them at a store in tiny Orcutt, trading the critters for $21 and a quantity of Hostetter's Bitters. They next stole a blooded horse, which was later recovered. It wasn't much of a crime wave thus far, but Buck, as the ringleader, had to interrupt his new career to do a short stretch in the Fort Smith jail for bringing whiskey into Indian Territory.

And there Buck met his idol, Crawford Goldsby, better known as Cherokee Bill, a hoodlum entirely without redeeming social value, the sort of professional outlaw Buck aspired to become. While Buck was in the slam, Cherokee Bill tried to break out and in the process killed a highly respected jailer.

Having learned nothing from his stint behind bars, Buck was then slapped on the wrist for a minor rustling crime, having graduated from hogs to cattle. He did not stand trial this time, however, snatching his guard's semiautomatic pistol and running away down the streets of Okmulgee. He was ready for the big time and he had his gang re-formed.

Early in the morning of July 29, 1895, a fire raged through the little town of Checotah, on the Katy railroad southeast of Okmulgee. The fire had begun in the livery stable and rapidly spread, and the whole town turned out to fight the flames, including an itinerant fire extinguisher salesman, who promptly put his stock to work. The townspeople managed to save the horses from the fire, but the stable was ruined. Surveying the damage, the stable owner noticed that all of the ironwork and most of the saddles were missing.

It then developed that somebody had stolen some fine horses from a nearby pasture and presumably had saddled them with the stolen horse furniture, setting fire to the stable to cover their crime. It was the Buck Gang, and things were only beginning to heat up.

Their next crime was the shooting of John Garrett, a black deputy US marshal, near the town of Okmulgee. The lawman was deliberately murdered because he knew the gang members for what they were—evil men with no remorse.

Garrett was hunting for Buck and went to Peterson's store because Buck's mother was there. As he went out to the back porch to see her, her son stepped out of hiding and shot him down; then Buck and the Davis boys mounted and galloped, whooping, out of town. According to a conflicting account, the marshal had been called to a robbery in progress at Peterson's and made the mistake of ordering Rufus Buck to throw up his hands. Instead, Buck turned on the marshal and shot him down.

Whether Buck alone killed the lawman, or other gang members helped him, all their names would quickly become synonymous with unbridled ferocity. They encountered a wagon driven by a man and his daughter. These were the odds Buck liked, and so he and his four henchmen stopped the wagon, ordered the daughter out of the wagon, and one by one raped her. The *Muskogee Phoenix* reported that the girl received "critical injuries." If the murder of the lawman had not been enough, this crime put the gang beyond the pale for all time. Having amused themselves brutalizing a young girl, the gang rode off for further adventures.

Next, on Berryhill Creek not far from Okmulgee, the five stopped and robbed Jim Staley. Staley was riding a high-class horse, and Buck offered to trade him for the animal. When Staley said he wasn't interested, Buck struck him in the head with his Winchester and knocked him bleeding from the saddle. Then the gang pretty well cleaned poor Staley out, taking his watch, $50, his fine horse, and horse furniture. But at least they left him alive, after a debate and a vote over whether and how to kill him. The vote was three to two, and by that narrow margin Staley lived.

The next victim was Bert Callahan, owner of the U-Bar Ranch on Grave Creek. The gang jumped Callahan and his hired hand, a black cowboy named Sam Houston, while the pair was returning to the ranch from Okmulgee, and opened fire without warning. Houston's horse was killed, and Houston ran for his life. Buck drove a bullet through Houston's lungs and then turned on Callahan, shooting a piece off one of his ears.

Callahan was the son of the superintendent of Wealaka Mission School, from which Buck had been ejected for causing disturbances. And Buck later said he saw Callahan and would have killed him if, at the time, he had known Callahan's identity.

The gang next tried a bit of nighttime horse thievery at Gus Chambers's home on Duck Creek in the area of Sapulpa. But Chambers was tough and he owned a shotgun, so what they got was not horses but gunfire, and the gang had to content themselves with riddling the Chambers' house with bullets while the farmer's family cowered under a bed. The Buck Gang appeared to have had no lack of ammunition because about a hundred shots were fired in the fight, eight of which struck the bed under which the family had taken refuge.

On August 5 the gang stopped two wagons, one of which was driven by Mrs. Mary Wilson, a widow moving her possessions from one farm to another. Accompanying her was her son Charles and a boy she had hired to help out. After Buck and his minions took what they wanted from Mrs. Wilson, they told the boys to drive on down the road. Davis then turned to the helpless woman, and after he had raped her, the gang drove her into the brush with gunfire, where later she was found by a posse, half dead from fright and abuse.

Later that same day they also robbed and murdered a man working on a ranch between Checotah and Okmulgee. That night they went to a house where a schoolteacher was boarding, stuck up everybody there, and raped the teacher.

As if these outrages were not enough, the next day the Buck Gang reached a new level of depravity, the Hassan rape. At Hassan's home between Snake and Duck Creeks, some twenty miles from Sapulpa, they rode into the yard and asked for water. Henry Hassan had been dozing under an arbor while his thirty-year-old wife, his mother-in-law, and his three small children peeled fruit nearby.

Hassan and Lewis Davis had had trouble before, when Hassan had asked him to close his gates after he passed through his land. Hassan recognized him now and knew he and his family were in the hands of the worst band of outlaws of the day. He tried to casually enter his house to get his rifle, but Maoma July beat him to it.

Buck was his usual boastful self, bragging that he was Cherokee Bill's brother—which he was not—and demanded that Mrs. Hassan and her mother cook them a dinner and be damned quick about it. The gang ransacked the house, stealing what pittance of money the Hassans had, and other trinkets and articles of clothing, including, of all things, baby dresses. They then stuffed their bellies with dinner and afterward amused themselves by raping Mrs. Hassan and brutalizing the family. When the gang disappeared with her husband, terrified Mrs. Hassan hid in a cornfield; her husband had been gone so long that she thought the outlaws had carried out their threat to murder him. Hassan was picked up by a passing neighbor and returned to his home, exhausted but safe. A posse appeared but could not pick up the gang's tracks until the next morning.

By now word of their depredations had spread, and dozens of men—Indian, white, and black—were on the gang's trail.

However, the Buck Gang was not through. Their next stop was Orcutt, where they invaded the local store and took their choice of its merchandise. The owner was gone, out with a posse hunting the gang, but he had had the foresight to take the store's cash along with him. His two young sons were minding the store. Fortunately, the gang paid no attention to the kids but looted the store of food and ammunition.

They went on to rob a Norbury and Company store, and there they got a little cash, a large quantity of ammunition and weapons, and still more food.

Their next stop, it seemed, would be Severs's store. Warned of the gang's impending arrival, the storekeeper at Severs hastened to hide the cash, swollen to nearly $20,000 because a payment had been made to the Indians and their accounts had been paid two or three days before. It was taken to the second floor of the building and stuffed into the pockets of some of the men's suits on display there.

In any event the gang did not appear at Severs's, but they were not through with little businesses and hit a grocery store in the village of McDermott. They were looking for cash, but they found none and vented their anger and disappointment by smashing the store owner's display furniture and covering the floor with his sugar and flour.

They finished their day by robbing still another store owner, leaving him tied up and poorer by a couple of sacks filled with merchandise.

The gang should have run, but it didn't. Now a host of hunters was on the trail, including Captain Harry and other officers of the Creek Lighthorse police, plus two deputy US marshals, heading a huge posse of angry citizens that may have numbered as many as one hundred. The gang's trail could not have been hard to follow, because soon the pursuers found the outlaws at Flat Rock, north of Okmulgee.

The outlaws were sitting in a circle in the shade of a grove of trees. They were intent on splitting up a heap of loot taken in the store robberies and were squabbling over who got what. Buck finally grew tired of the wrangling and told them he was in charge, and they'd get what he said they could have and nothing else. That fiat aroused considerable ill will, and they soon returned to fighting over the booty. However, the gang did not post a sentry on the high ground above them, from which an alert man could have spotted the posse before it closed in.

And so the wrangling over the loot continued, until the posse opened fire. Men on the trail of rapists in that faraway time understandably did not assign a high priority to due process of law, but somehow the first volley missed the outlaws. The gang could not reach their horses, however, and so they grabbed their weapons and scrambled to the top of the little hill.

The firing was heavy and one of the outlaw's rounds went through Lighthorse Captain Harry's hat, creasing his skull and knocking him off his horse. Once Harry had shaken off the shock of the bullet, he turned out to be unwounded and went back into the fight.

For a while the situation was a stalemate because the outlaws had the advantage of fighting from the high ground, but they were heavily outnumbered by the posse. Messengers galloped off all the way to Fort Smith to spread the news, while the lawmen began to crawl up the hill slowly under a broiling sun.

At Fort Smith the first reports told of a furious battle and even of fighting hand to hand. Judge Parker, apparently imperturbable, carried on with his crowded docket while excitement in the streets of the town rose higher and higher. The courtroom was abuzz, too, and from time to time Judge Parker had to call for order. Crowds milled about in the streets of the town, waiting for news.

Meanwhile, around the little knoll bullets flew back and forth for seven hours, without anybody on either side being hurt at all. But as the men of the posse inched up the slopes of the hill, they knew that in the end they had only to wait, for they could resupply their ammunition while the Bucks could not. But the fighting kept on, and sooner or later posse members would work their way far enough up the sides of the little hill that they could rush the gang at close range.

And even more help was on the way. Marshal S. Martin Rutherford was hurrying from Muskogee with another posse, arriving about sundown to see the coming evening flickering with the flash of muzzle blasts and a pall of smoke hanging over the hilltop. Rutherford's posse would ensure that nobody was going to escape.

As night began to fall, the lawmen worked in closer and closer, shooting at muzzle flashes in the gathering darkness. Soon a Euchee Indian posse man grew tired of lying on his belly exchanging fire with the gang. He rose to his feet and fired a dynamite cartridge, a rifle round with a bit of explosive jammed into a cavity in the tip of the bullet, at the hilltop. This round exploded against a tree on the hill, and a fragment cut through Buck's cartridge belt. He threw down his rifle and turned away to flee. His companions panicked too, and the whole gang took to their heels over the rear of the rise, straight into the arms of Rutherford's men. The hoodlums had had enough and did not try to resist.

Buck, Maoma July, and Luckey Davis were immediately apprehended. Both Lewis Davis—who had a bullet hole in one leg—and Sam Sampson managed to hide from the posse and remained free.

The prisoners were loaded down with chains and taken into tiny McDermott, where relieved Creek people appeared from all directions to see these unspeakable scum who had murdered and raped and terrified decent people. Marshal Rutherford of the Northern District was in command now, and he was understandably worried about the continued life of his prisoners. Crowds had gathered in the streets, and there was a great deal of murmuring about lynching.

Rutherford went out to speak to the crowd and promised that the outlaws would be taken to Fort Smith and tried in Judge Parker's dreaded court. There would be justice, he said and reminded the town that he was duty bound to defend the prisoners. He would do it, he told them, and reminded the crowd that all of his men would shoot straight. "The life of one of you is not worth the lives of all of them," he told the crowd.

For a while things quieted down, but then men began to remember federal criticisms about Creek indifference to law enforcement in the Nation, and once again the temper of the town turned sour. The mob began to post guards to make sure the marshals and their charges did not slip away in the darkness.

Rutherford could see what was coming, and he knew he had to get his prisoners out of town to avoid a lynching or a firefight or both. "Now," said the marshal to the prisoners, "you have a chance to save your own lives. We are going to try to escape this mob, but we can't have your chains clanking in the gloom. If they do, you will probably die on the nearest tree right here in town. So pick up your chains and carry them and keep them from rattling if you value your lives at all." They did, and for about half a mile, lawmen and prisoners moved stealthily away from the murmuring mob.

Rutherford's caution paid off, because in the darkness he got his charges to Muskogee without incident, then onto a train to Fort Smith. They would live a little longer.

In Fort Smith the gang was led down Garrison Avenue to the government barracks enclosure, then across it to the jail. There the gang disappeared into cells to await trial, while the lawyers for both sides prepared their cases and witnesses were called to Fort Smith. The grand jury returned a true bill on the indictment of the gang for the rape of Rosetta Hassan, and, on August 20, they were arraigned before Judge Parker.

After the fight at the hilltop, Lewis Davis had gotten clear and reached the home of the Richardson family, where he hoped to hide. It was not long, however, before his leg wound began to go bad, apparently from blood poisoning. Mr. Richardson got word out to the law, and officers converged on the Richardson place. They did not have long to wait. Davis came out of the house, carrying his rifle, and started washing his wound. But when he straightened up and reached for his weapon, it was gone.

Richardson had taken the rifle, and the law moved in and led Davis down the road to Fort Smith. There he joined the rest of the gang behind bars, and doctors treated his wound, which turned out to be minor. Along with Buck and Luckey Davis, he was indicted for the Garrett murder, and he joined all of the gang under indictment for the attempted murder of Sam Houston and rape of Mrs. Hassan.

At trial Assistant US Attorney J. B. McDonough had plenty of ammunition. He led off with Hassan and Ryan, whose testimony was damning enough. But then Mrs. Hassan took the stand. The courtroom was dead silent while Mrs. Hassan testified. There was, a reporter wrote, "scarcely a dry eye" in the jury box, and women in the courtroom cried in sympathy for the lady on the stand. Even tough Judge Parker was seen to wipe his eyes.

Mrs. Hassan left the stand without cross-examination, the lawyers "standing aside and bowing reverently," as she passed. After that there was no doubt of the verdict. When it came time for final argument, one of the appointed defense counsel simply announced to the jury and Judge Parker, "May it please the court and you gentlemen of the jury, I have nothing to say." There wasn't much else he could say. And prosecutor McDonough passed up argument as well, simply telling the jurors that they had heard the evidence and he would expect a conviction. He got one for all five of the gang. It took three minutes. The jury did not even sit down to deliberate.

Parker then excused that jury and seated a new one. This time the charge was the murder of Marshal Garrett, of which Rufus Buck and the two Davises stood accused. Buck tried to offer an alibi, saying he wasn't there, he was someplace else. The jury wasn't having any of the alibi, and this time they returned in just twelve minutes with a verdict of guilty for all three men.

Judge Parker delayed sentencing for two more days, and then the gang faced the stern judge. Parker addressed Rufus Buck's case first, adding to the legal language a lecture for the soul of the gang's leader, something he often did when announcing sentence.

The verdict is an entirely just one, and one that must be approved by all lovers of virtue. . . . The Lawmakers of the United States have deemed your offense equal in enormity and wickedness to murder. It has been proven beyond question.

And then, to nobody's surprise, devout Judge Parker sentenced Buck to hang and added, "May God, whose laws you have broken, and before whose tribunal you must appear, have mercy on your soul."

The other outlaws got the same sentence. They were first asked whether they had anything to say, as was the custom. Only Luckey Davis responded. "Yes," he said. "I want my case to go up to the Supreme Court."

"I don't blame you," replied the judge, continuing his long and forbidding sentencing speech. "This horrible crime now rests upon your souls. Remove it if you can so the good God of all will extend you His forgiveness and His mercy."

Execution was delayed while Buck's lawyer lodged an appeal with the US Supreme Court, which under a curious jurisdictional anomaly was the direct appellate authority over the Western District of Arkansas. Buck's claim on appeal was again that he could have produced evidence giving himself an alibi, had he been allowed additional time to prepare for trial. The Supreme Court was not impressed.

NO HOPE NOW, read the headline in the *Muskogee Phoenix* of June 26, 1896. THE BUCK GANG WILL HANG TOGETHER NEXT WEEK.

Buck created a curious document while he was awaiting execution. He had found religion, apparently, or pretended he did. In a letter to his wife, he enclosed a bit of crude poetry, full of misspellings and scribbled on the back of a picture of his mother. It included a rough drawing of a cross planted firmly in the Rock of Ages. On the cross he printed, "Holy Ghost, Father, Son," and down below it, "Virtue and Resurrection" and "Remember Me."

The *Muskogee Phoenix* called the drawing "really clever," something of an exaggeration, and announced that "it makes a splendid photograph, and for those who wish curious mementoes of outlaws and other people, will no doubt be much sought after."

And so, on July 1, 1896, the Buck Gang was led out to the monstrous five-rope gibbet, said to be the largest in the United States, and there they were put down on a bench to reflect on what was about to happen next. A priest who had ministered to the defendants in jail said a prayer, and Rufus Buck's father tried to climb up to the gibbet platform. He was stumbling drunk, however, and lawmen barred his way.

Marshal George Crump formally read the death warrants. Then he turned to the gang members and asked, as was the custom of the time, whether any of them had any last words. A couple of them called out to people in the audience, but otherwise they were silent. Except for Lewis Davis, that is, who made the curious request that he be hanged alone. The marshal wouldn't allow it, and all that was left to do was get on with the execution.

And when the trap dropped, the good people of eastern Indian Territory breathed a little easier and slept better that night. The *Fort Smith Elevator* reported the demise of the gang under a brief and descriptive headline: FIVE STRUNG UP.

Al Spencer
Prince of Fumblers

Al Spencer came from a good family, born near Lenapah in Oklahoma, the day after Christmas, 1887. He started out in honest work as a farmer and cowboy, but by 1916 he was in trouble with the law: The charge was cattle rustling. He did some more stock rustling after that, plus some automobile rustling as well, until in 1919 he and two others burglarized a store up in Neodesha, Kansas.

This time the law recovered most of the booty, and Al too. He sent a telegram to a friend asking him to send money to a place in Colorado. Agents from the Burns Detective Agency read his mail, and when Al went to the post office to pick up his money, he found a set of handcuffs instead. The Kansas crime got him five years.

He was still charged with rustling in Oklahoma at the time, however, so back there he went. Pleading guilty, he got a stretch at the McAlester penitentiary.

In any case Al got out and went back to what he liked to do: take things that belonged to other folks. Al was his usual inept self. After rustling some more cars, he is supposed to have stuck up the assistant postmaster of a small town as the postmaster was walking home from a poker game. This got Al some serious time, fourteen years back in McAlester, where he became a trusty.

In 1921 or early in 1922, Al disappeared from prison for quite some time. He was assisted in his departure by Henry Wells, a fellow inmate. When somebody asked where Al was, Wells told prison guards Al was probably drinking off in a choc joint where trustees often went, choc being a sort of beer. The authorities accepted that Al was taking advantage of this curious custom, which bought Al enough time to get away, and back he went to his outlaw career. This time he would concentrate on banks.

In December 1921 a former friend named Silas Meigs held up the bank in Nelagony, a hamlet on the fringe of the Osage Hills in northeastern Oklahoma. He got some $1,500 single-handedly and galloped off on horseback, eluding the posse chasing him. Al, just out of McAlester, soon joined him. Together they robbed a bank in Pawhuska, taking away a paltry $147.60. Then, still in February, they hit the bank in Broken Bow, and this time they struck it rich, taking in something between $6,000 and $7,000. They forced a local man to drive them out of town to a spot where they had stashed their horses. Then they galloped away, eluding another posse.

They hid out for a while with Sol Wells up in Al's favorite stomping ground, the tangled wilderness of the Osage Hills. It was tough country, thick with scrub oak and interlaced with arroyos and covered with brush.

Al and Meigs must have felt secure as well as smug, but that was not to last, because a posse came upon them at Wells's place. The lawmen weren't looking for them, just stalking a still somewhere in the area, but as they neared the outlaws' lair, Meigs shot and killed a posse man. The return fire hit and killed Meigs, the first of a number of Al's associates who would finish their earthly course on the wrong end of a bullet.

Not being daunted by the death of Meigs, Al teamed up with Henry Wells and a couple of other outlaws, Jay Majors and Slim Connelly. They set their sights on a bank in little Pineville, Missouri, in the spring of 1922. Then they robbed a local bootlegger, which brought out the law. On suspicion, the law stopped a car carrying three men and a woman, Eva Evers.

The officers were immediately in a gunfight with the occupants, and, in the exchange of shots, Majors, a passenger, took a round in the groin. But the officers were driven away. The outlaws dropped Majors off at a Joplin hospital where, not surprisingly, the law soon found him. They also found Eva and arrested her as well.

Al got away, rode a freight train to safety, and eventually made it to the Osage Hills. About now Connelly quit the gang, only to be replaced by young Dick Gregg, son of a hardcase father who a couple of years later would shoot and kill a notorious outlaw, one Poffenberger. Dick Gregg fit right in.

In early June 1922 the outlaws' next venture started as the burglary of a store in Ochelata, but this time they were stopped by the night marshal, William Lockett. The bandits ended his interference by killing Lockett. One of them was quoted as saying, "You've followed us long enough, you old bastard."

The Elgin State Bank, just over the border in Kansas, was a better strike. There the gang got about $2,000 in cash, plus a bundle of bonds with a face value of some $20,000. Then, at the end of July, four outlaws hit the Citizens' Bank of Lenapah—Al's hometown—and got away with about $1,300. The robbers wore masks, but the odds are that it was Al and his hoodlums on the prowl again.

They got another $3,000 or so at Centralia in September. They'd added another gang member, Ralph Carter. Carter had the misfortune to encounter three veteran officers looking for a still, however, and tried to shoot it out with them. He lost.

By now Al had been identified as part of the gang, but that didn't stop him or the others. In October of 1922 he was part of a bank robbery at Osage. This time there were five robbers, and two of them were women (or men dressed as women). It is a subject of some debate, but this may have been the first appearance of Goldie Bates, Al's girlfriend.

On October 18 the bank at Dewey lost some $2,500 to three bandits, who locked the bank personnel in the vault. The robbers were spotted in a fast Hudson Speedster, allegedly driven by a woman who could have been Goldie. They got away clean.

Until, that is, one of the bank employees picked Henry Wells out of a photo lineup. But Wells offered an alibi backed up by witnesses, and when he was tried, his lawyer got a hung jury.

For law-abiding people, worse was to follow. On October 20 Majors and other prisoners broke out of the Vinita jail while a revival meeting was in progress nearby. They disappeared into the night in stolen cars.

Later in October Al and two others hit the bank in Talala for approximately $1,200, fleeing back to the wilds of the Osage. By now Al had recruited some more bad hats, a juvenile delinquent named Ralph Clopton and Emmett Daugherty, said to be related to the dean of bank robbers, Henry Starr. Also added to the pack was Dick Gregg's buddy Lee Clingan. About a month later three gang members got more cash from the Caddo National Bank down in Oklahoma. Later that December the gang got themselves some Christmas presents at a jewelry store up in Kansas, fleeing in their by-now-familiar Hudson Speedster. This time they struck it rich, by their standards at least, by making off with jewelry and watches worth as much as $20,000.

But the day after Christmas, a posse rounded up Majors. In the spring he would be sentenced to a prison term of twenty-one years. About this time Al was approached by William Hale, the grey eminence behind the notorious murders of Indian oil-rights holders up in the Osage. The story goes that Hale wanted Al to do some of Hale's killing for him, but the outlaw declined. That stands to his credit, or maybe he just thought it would be too risky or the pay was too small.

Robberies followed at banks in Virgil and Cambridge, Kansas. After the Cambridge raid the gang hastened to find sanctuary down in Oklahoma, driving across fields and through fences on the way. Inevitably they got stuck in a tangle of fence wire, and, when they tried to free themselves, a pursuing posse shot up the car and wounded Clopton, Daughterty, and a hostage.

Now a prisoner, Clopton lost no time in telling the law that Al was the gang leader. Clopton got fifteen years in prison and that finished his outlaw career. After this latest debacle the gang hid out for a month or so, then robbed another Kansas bank. Wells was arrested for this one, but bank employees could not identify him as one of the robbers.

In March things turned really ugly. In Bartlesville an automobile passed the home of police chief Gaston, and somebody fired on the house. It was Al, although he was not identified as the shooter until much later. In the same month the gang hit a bank in Mannford, west of Tulsa, taking a disappointing $600.

They were pursued by a posse and had to abandon their car when they blew a tire. One of the outlaws, a Tulsa man called Leo Sturtz, was captured while he was trying vainly to change the tire. And the next day still another outlaw went down in a firefight with lawmen. The dead bandit turned out to be Bud

139

Maxfield, a veteran badman who in years past had ridden with Henry Starr.

The gang's next raid was into Arkansas, where they robbed the bank in Gentry, close to the Oklahoma border, driving one car and leaving another just across the line in Oklahoma. The idea was that they would flee Gentry in one car, return to Oklahoma for a second one, and head for the tall timber on horseback.

About this time Al rented a farm over in Delaware County, Oklahoma, leaving it in the custody of his half brother Campbell Keys. Keys, Al told the property owner, needed to live away from civilization for a time, because he was a recovering junkie. Once provided with a sanctuary, the gang went after the Gentry bank. Al's crew now included Wells, Big Boy Berry, Nick Lamar, and Ralph White, with Si Fogg as horse holder.

And so, on March 31, 1923, Al and the gang arrived in Gentry driving a stolen Studebaker. While White waited behind the wheel of the car, the other three went inside, held up bank personnel, and snatched a little over $2,000. But a bank employee hit the silent alarm, and while the gang headed for the car, citizens with guns converged on the bank. Bullets began to fly, and Al and his boys ran for it.

The gang roared out of town, right into an ambush two or three miles down the road. Firing from behind a stone wall in a small village, lawmen and citizens drilled Lamar in the shoulder and legs, White in his arms and side, and Al in one arm. The car was riddled, but the outlaws got to their stashed horses and rode away.

The bandits went to ground in a cemetery from which Al walked into a town and telephoned Stanley Snyder in

Bartlesville. Snyder and another man picked up the battered outlaws and drove them back to safety up in the Osage.

In the next few months, more robberies were committed in the general vicinity of the Osage, but whether Al was involved is unknown. But then on the night of April 16, the gang hit the post office in Pawhuska, a number of men and two women parking in front of their target. They threw down on a deputy US marshal named Tom Walton as he walked over to talk to them, then forced a cab driver down on the pavement beside the lawman. Some of the men stood guard while the others broke into the post office.

All was quiet until two citizens passed. Unsuspecting, the men were walking peacefully homeward in the darkness when one of the bandits yelled at the two, then cut "Shorty" Harrison down with a shotgun blast. Bob Wilkerson tried to draw his pistol but went down before a second shotgun blast.

One of the women saw the outlaw's stupid act for what it was: disaster. "You ignorant bastard," she yelled, "you've shot two innocent men and now there'll be hell to pay."

About then the night lit up with a colossal explosion inside the post office building. The outlaws had dynamited the post office safe, using a charge heavy enough to hurl the outer safe door some thirty feet. But it appeared that Al and his cohorts weren't very good at handling explosives, because the explosion also jammed the safe's inner door so tight that it sealed off the contents of the safe. The robbers got nothing. They ran then, spraying bullets indiscriminately in all directions, leaped into their cars, and roared off toward Bartlesville.

Wilkerson died later that night when doctors could not halt the bleeding from his torn femoral artery. He was in his early twenties, and the next day would have been his wedding day. Harrison survived. Officers from all over joined in the hunt: Robbery was one thing; cold-blooded murder was quite another.

The following day the law hit pay dirt near Ochelata. While two officers were questioning the people living there, one of the bandits opened fire on them from his hiding place in an attic. A return volley from the lawmen produced the almost instant surrender of a thug known as Ed Shull, and another who was shot through the leg, Clarence Ward. The two had an arsenal in the house, and Shull was already wanted for assault on an officer and suspected in two robberies.

Frightened of being lynched—a well-founded fear—Shull spilled his guts. On his information lawmen raided Sol Wells's home, where they put the arm on Earl Holman. Holman would get thirty years, and Shull five, his lighter sentence a thank-you for the information he had furnished. Clarence Ward, who lost his leg to amputation, was charged with the Caddo bank robbery.

Ironically, though the civilized world was well rid of Shull and company, they may not have been involved in the post office raid. That was attributed to Al and his gang, and Al himself was identified as the probable killer of Wilkerson.

At last on April 21, Al was spotted in a stolen car with a woman and three other men. A posse ran down the automobile, loaded with weapons and camping equipment but now abandoned, and not far away they splattered gang member Nick Lamar with buckshot and arrested him.

Then on May 4 Texas lawmen stopped a stolen car and arrested Goldie Bates, Al's girlfriend, plus Big Boy Berry and

Carl Priss. Priss was described as a Texas horse thief. Goldie and Priss were later released, there being no valid charges against them. Lamar and Berry, having admitted participation in the Gentry robbery, got some serious prison time from the court in Benton County, Arkansas, as did sometime gang members Keyes and Reasor, for the same crime.

Instead of running for safety, leaving Oklahoma, or holing up in the Osage, Al took on a train. He was accompanied by Frank "Jelly" Nash, longtime criminal Earl Thayer, and a small army of other outlaws. Included were Riley Dixon, Curtis Kelly, Grover Durrill, and Whitey Fallon (born plain old George Curtis).

Al's band of boobies had earlier demonstrated their intellectual poverty by driving around western Arkansas with a jug of nitroglycerine, covered with a blanket, sitting on the running board of their car. Suddenly discovering that the blanket was inexplicably on fire, they got rid of the explosive. But Al pressed on with his plan, having been told that a shipment of Liberty Bonds was on the way to Oklahoma City from Muskogee. The place chosen to stop their target was Okesa, a tiny spot on the Katy line.

Early in the morning of August 21, the train stopped briefly to let off a passenger, and the gang struck. The fireman was beaten and ordered to cut the engine and baggage car loose from the rest of the train. Bleeding, the man did so and then was forced to sit with the engineer and two mail clerks.

There wasn't much in the express safe, but the robbers did get the Liberty Bonds, plus some money out of the registered mail and a couple of thousand in cash. But they couldn't get in to rob the passengers, thanks to the Pullman porter, a tough black man named T. J. Davis. Davis got the coach doors locked and tried to find somebody among the passengers who had a gun. Nobody did, or at least nobody would admit he did. Davis was disgusted and said so: "I suppose they were all from Kansas. They sure wasn't from Oklahoma, or they would all have had gats."

The bandits climbed into three autos and roared away into the night. Their satisfaction with an unusually large haul would not last long.

There is a persistent story that on this job Al won a brief measure of fame as the man who used rubber fingerstalls to frustrate the burgeoning art of fingerprint identification. Al figured his ploy would keep his fingerprints off anything he touched during another robbery of a Katy train. It did. But what he didn't figure on were some bright Katy detectives who asked around to find out who'd been buying lots of fingerstalls.

The story seems to be true, except that the notion came from one of Al's confederates— an oaf called Ike Ogg. Ogg was quickly arrested and began to rat forthwith.

The law swept up a passel of well-known Osage badmen and also netted Goldie Bates again, who was taken to Pawhuska dressed in red stockings beneath a short dress. Goldie was feisty as always, fighting the officers who arrested her. While nearly all of those arrested would later be released as not being involved in the train holdup, Ogg pleaded guilty.

Officers got Earl Thayer at home in Oklahoma City and netted Curtis Kelly on August 30. Kelly gave the lawmen all the information they needed, and by September 8 the world was told the names of the gang members, given their descriptions, and advised that each carried a substantial reward, whether dead or alive. Al was named, as was Riley "Pug" Dixon, Grover Durrill, Jelly Nash, and Whitey Fallon.

On September 15 US Marshal Alva McDonald led a posse to ambush along a road they had been told Al would use. It was a rainy night, and the officers—including Luther Bishop, the most famous and lethal cop of his time—huddled in the darkness waiting for their target to appear. It was a long wait, but finally they saw Al crossing a bridge and moving in their direction.

McDonald said that he ordered Al to surrender, but the outlaw fired twice in the darkness. The posse's return fire punctured Al eight times. As usual, there were a number of versions of precisely what happened on that gloomy road, but there was no argument with the fact that Al was very dead.

Some people speculated that the lawmen had killed Al in Kansas. Others said it happened in Oklahoma. Whatever happened, he remained dead.

He was planted in a cemetery outside Nowata, on a soggy day in September. For all his notoriety nobody cared enough to come. Only his wife, daughter, and sister showed up to say good-bye.

Part of the sequel was the conviction of Fallon, Thayer, Durrill, and Curtis Kelly, Stanley Snyder beat his wife once too often, and in 1926 she filled him full of a fatal dose of bullets. Dick Gregg got ten to twenty up in Kansas but escaped and went back to robbing again. He got some help and hit some more banks, then capped his ugly career not far from Tulsa by shooting down two Oklahoma highway patrolmen. One of the officers killed Gregg in the gunfight, but both troopers would die.

Other leftovers of Al's gang broke out of prison in 1931. With some other prisoners, Earl Thayer, Grover Durrill, and

Whitey Fallon reached freedom—briefly—and then managed to make every mistake they possibly could, including getting their car stuck and failing in their attempts to hijack two more. Their escape attempt fell apart within ten miles of the prison.

Four of the escapees, including Thayer, took refuge in a farmhouse, which was soon surrounded by as many as two hundred law officers. Three of the escapees went upstairs and tried to make a fight of it, but there was no place to hide, no way to run. After a lengthy bombardment, the officers cautiously approached the farmhouse to find Durrill, Fallon, and a third man, Green, all quite dead, apparently suicides.

The canny Thayer had bailed out a back window early in the action, but his success was fleeting. He attracted the suspicion of a couple of civilians who pulled a gun on him and called the police. Back to prison he went, where he died in July of 1934.

And so passed Al Spencer and the gaggle of losers called the Spencer Gang, either into prison or into the grave.

None of them ever learned a thing.

The Caseys and the Christians
Brother Acts

The men boarded the train when it stopped at little Pond Creek for water. They threw down on the train crew and forced them to stop, at which time the rest of the gang, brandishing loaded shotguns and bad tempers, came out of the darkness running and shooting.

Inside the express car were express messenger John Crosswight and the guard, Jake Harmon. At first the two did not yield to demands to open the express car. But then the bandits planted dynamite at the car door and fired it off. The door remained closed, although the express packages were scattered around the car and Crosswight was stunned. "Open up," yelled voices outside, "or we'll throw explosives right on you." Crosswight opened the door.

Meanwhile, Harmon had slipped out, back through the cars behind the express car, emerging into the night with his trusty shotgun. He spotted three outlaws shouting orders to the engineer and fireman and nailed one of them with a load of buckshot. The bandit went down and stayed down, and his companions panicked, ran to their horses, and clattered off into the night.

About this time a Pond Creek posse showed up. The posse ran down one outlaw as he fled madly down a road. He told them he was just a hobo hitching a ride, but he was clanking with weaponry, gave several names, and convinced nobody. The other bandits were at large and still unknown.

147

This robbery actually had its beginnings earlier when Zip Wyatt turned his attention back to Oklahoma and recruited several other men, including two brothers. A pair of suspicious-looking characters appeared in the little town of El Reno on May 21 and seemed to be giving particular attention to the jail. The local sheriff was suspicious, and when the two left town, a deputy trailed them. They had told the deputy they hailed from Chickasha and were bound for Enid, but when they left town, they headed along the railroad line toward Yukon.

The deputy saw the two signal to someone on a passing train, and when the train reached El Reno, it was found to be carrying none other than the harridan wife of Nate Sylva, who had also been swept into the bag by the law. It looked as if an escape attempt was in the making. The local sheriff wired Yukon to alert deputy Sam Farris there, and Farris found the suspicious-looking pair and told them they were under arrest.

One of them wheeled on Farris and shot him in the groin. The deputy was able to draw and return the fire, and one of his bullets hit an outlaw in the foot. As Farris fell dying, the wounded outlaw hobbled away while his companion, spraying bullets, ran for their horses. The wounded hoodlum did not get far, because Farris's brother ran into the street and tackled him, holding on until other citizens could run to help.

At this the second outlaw opened fire on Farris's brother and the others, and one round ricocheted from a nearby mowing machine and fatally wounded a bystander, an old man named Snyder. But when a citizen opened fire on the mounted outlaw and when the outlaw saw other citizens beginning to gather weapons, he galloped out of town, abandoning his companion.

A big posse was right behind him, but they lost him in darkness among the thickets along the South Canadian River.

Yukon citizens were understandably angry, and so the wounded outlaw was moved to the guardhouse at Fort Reno as a precaution against an impromptu necktie party. He would not give his name, but Deputy Marshal Chris Madsen saw him and knew him immediately as Vic Casey. Soon authorities realized that the escapee was his brother, James Casey, and the hunt was on.

Madsen gathered a posse and picked up the fugitive's trail in the brakes of the South Canadian. The pursuit covered just over a hundred miles, ending predictably at the Caseys' new place out west of the town of Arapaho. The posse swept up James Casey and turned for home.

Both Caseys denied any wrongdoing, but it wouldn't do either one of them any good. Vic's foot wound got worse and worse until blood poisoning set in, eventually killing him. His brother's lawyer moved for a change of venue to Oklahoma County, and he was moved there in 1894. He ended up sharing a cell with the brothers Christian, whose names belied their dispositions.

The Caseys were just plain rotten, but it's hard to assign a specific reason to why the Christian boys went sour. In 1891 brothers Bill and Bob migrated with their family from Texas into the wide-open land north of the Canadian River, in what was to become Pottawatomie County, Oklahoma Territory. This wild and woolly area was studded with "saloon towns," wide spots in the road like Young's Crossing, Keokuk Falls, Violet Springs, and the Corner, a tiny patch of land on the South Canadian River where several low-class saloons attracted the trash of the territory.

Violence was a way of life down here: The booze parlors of Keokuk Falls were aptly known as the seven deadly saloons. At the Corner lived a very patient doctor named Mooney, who treated dozens of casualties from gunshots, knifings, and other violent batteries, once doing an amputation on a saloon table while a drunk held a lamp to light the doctor's work and revelry continued all around him.

The county became a ready-made haven for career outlaws like the Daltons, Bill Doolin, Zip Wyatt, and the Casey boys. It also provided sanctuary for inept amateur bandits like Al Jennings, and for a horde of small-time punks. With Indian Territory on two sides, the county was ideal as a base for the bootleggers who ran prohibited hooch into the Indian lands. It was here that the term *bootlegger* may have had its genesis, describing those smugglers who rode into Indian country with pint bottles of John Barleycorn stuffed into the tops of their boots.

But a lot of good people also lived here. The Pottawatomie country was known as a fine chance for the poor man, where crops grew well and game abounded, and where one little town was even named Moral, for its first citizen decreed no booze would be tolerated in his peaceful community. In and around Moral, the Anti-Horsethief Association did what it could to curb rampant livestock theft, decreeing that all horses must be branded with a "C" on the left jaw and have papers.

At first the Christian family was numbered among the honest folk. The brothers proved to be black sheep, however, and, by the time Bob was in his mid-twenties and Bill a mite younger, they had won an early and unenviable reputation as whiskey runners and horse thieves. In those days the Christian boys spent a good deal of time in Andy Morrison's saloon in Violet Springs. Andy was eventually murdered while sleeping in his own back room. About then the family moved north into Canadian County. In 1895 the brothers graduated from small-time crime to killing.

The brothers and a drinking buddy, John Mackey, walked out of Doug Barnes's saloon and found the law waiting for them. Deputy Will Turner had warrants for the arrest of the Christians, and he was tough enough to try to bring them in single-handed. Turner didn't count on the brothers and Mackey all drawing on him at once. He died in the dusty street. Tough sheriff W. B. "Billy" Trousdale ran down Mackey, and the Christian boys turned themselves in, which turned out to be a bad idea. The court reporter who recorded the case remembered that a "horde of people attended from the Four Corners District, and were about the hardest looking lot in my experience." The brothers were convicted and transferred to the Oklahoma County Jail in Oklahoma City, which in those days was a two-story building fitted with interior steel cages and considered a secure lockup.

Because neither James Casey—with whom they were sharing accommodations—nor the Christians were happy in jail, Bob Christian prevailed upon Jessie Finlay, his girlfriend, to smuggle in several guns, which he stashed in the stovepipe inside his cell. The outlaws chose Sunday, June 30, 1895, to make their break, because on Sundays, jailer J. H. Garver allowed his prisoners to move about in the corridor outside their cells. Garver was an easygoing sort, or maybe just plain negligent, because only the day before the Pottawatomie law had wired him, warning about the jailbreak.

The break started when Casey and the Christians pistol-whipped the jailer and ran into an alley behind the jail. There one of the Christians, probably Bill, stole a horse belonging to the police chief, Milt Jones, and galloped out of town. The other brother, Bob, and Casey fled on foot, stopped a couple in a buggy, and shoved their pistols into the driver's face. Carpenter Gus White, the driver, would not let loose of the reins and managed to pull the horses to a halt. Although the fugitives shot White in the leg and the stomach, he survived.

Chief Jones was closing in on the fugitives, however, and as he got within eight or ten feet of the buggy, one of the outlaws turned and shot him. Some observers thought a Christian killed the lawman, but the coroner's jury decided it was Casey. Whoever fired the shot, Jones staggered to the sidewalk and sank down against a building. He lived only five minutes after being shot.

A small war followed along Grand Avenue, pitting the fugitives against police officers Stafford and Jackson and several armed citizens. The lawmen drilled Casey through the neck and head, and the desperado died in White's riddled buggy.

Other citizens sprinted for cover. One went down with a leg wound, and a woman was slightly wounded by what the *Daily Oklahoman* called "a spent bullet," but otherwise the local folks, except for Gus White, escaped unharmed.

Not the case with the outlaws. In addition to Casey's fatal wound, Bob Christian was also hit but managed to run off down Grand Avenue until he met blacksmith Frank Berg, who was driving a cart. Christian robbed Berg of his cart, whipped up the horse, and clattered off to stick up another driver and hijack a faster team.

With Chief Jones dead in the street and both of the Christian brothers on the run, a posse of citizens equipped with bloodhounds pursued the outlaws. The *Daily Oklahoman* opined that there was "little doubt" the fugitives would be captured. "Should they be caught," the paper editorialized, "a double lynching will surely follow," which was a pretty fair prediction.

The Christian brothers were on the run, but they did not leave the area for the next couple of months. Even as lawmen sought their trail, the bandits embarked on a string of small-time raids on country post offices and general stores.

On July 28 the robbers held up the Wewoka Trading Company, the richest institution in the Seminole Nation. They left with only a couple of hundred dollars in provisions and equipment, because the only man who knew the safe combination had gone home for dinner.

Other raids on local stores followed until, on August 9, the brothers, with some equally evil cohorts, ran into an ambush near Wilburton. Deputy Marshal F. J. Stockton killed gang member John Fessenden, and gang member Foster Holbrook was captured. On August 21 outlaw John Reeves—one of those who had furnished weapons for the Oklahoma City jailbreak— was arrested near the town of Paoli. Later tried as a conspirator in Chief Jones's murder, he was sentenced to life.

On August 23 the Christians shot their way past lawmen west of Purcell. Although Deputy Marshall W. E. Hocker was wounded in the fight, the pursuing posse believed Hocker had gotten a bullet into Bob Christian. And then in the wee hours of September 30, Louis Miller—another of the jailbreak conspirators—was jumped by lawmen near Violet Springs. Miller decided to fight, but he came in second.

The gang reappeared in Oklahoma County in early September, breaking into the railroad agent's quarters in Edmond. And on October 6 they held up a St. Louis and San Francisco train east of Wilburton but rode off with only another measly haul. Their last hurrah came in December when they robbed a mining company store in Coalgate. This raid was still another poor payday: a little over $200 in cash, plus goods to the value of another $200 or so.

The territory had proved most unprofitable and downright dangerous. A month or so later, the Christian boys turned up in Seven Rivers, New Mexico. The brothers ended up in Arizona's Sulphur Springs Valley; by this time Bill was calling himself Ed Williams, while brother Bob adopted the handle of Tom Anderson.

Bill went to work breaking horses for the 4-Bar ranch and soon acquired the handle of "Black Jack" because of his dark hair and mustache (not to be confused with Black Jack Ketchum, for whom Christian is sometimes mistaken). His partner, an honest cowboy named Ed Wilson, said of Christian that "a finer partner never lived. Big, strong, fearless and good natured . . . ever ready to take his part, no matter what the game might be."

That is, when he wasn't trying to rob and kill people.

However, Christian soon raised another gang, including Texan Cole (or Code) Young. Then there was Bob Hayes, who may have been another Texan, or perhaps an Iowa hoodlum named Sam Hassels. Other gang members were veteran outlaw George Musgrave, another Texan, who also called himself Jeff Davis; Jesse Johnson; Jesse Williams; and one "Tom Anderson," who was probably brother Bob Christian. The gang became known in the southwest as the "High Fives," after a card game popular at the time.

With these trusty henchmen, and another hard case called Three-Fingered Jack Dunlap, on August 6, 1896, Black Jack rode off to rob the bank at Nogales, right on the border. Some of his band stayed outside with the horses; the others—probably Jesse Williams and Bob Hayes—went into the bank. They had excellent luck at first: Their mouths must have watered at the sight of some $30,000 in hard money, counted out and waiting for a rancher closing a stock purchase.

But here began the slow end of the outlaw careers of the Christian boys. Clerk Frank Herrera, all wool and a yard wide, snatched a pistol and began to blaze away. He didn't hit anybody, but his heroics were enough to drive the bandits pell-mell out into the street without their loot. This convinced the gang that Nogales was no place to tarry.

The gang struck the San Simon railroad station, and both the post office and Wickersham's Store at Bowie. But on a moonless night in October, the High Fives hit the eastbound Atlantic and Pacific train at the Rio Puerco trestle. The robbery should have been easy, for the train obligingly stopped while the engineer inspected a faulty piston rod. The gang shot the brakeman in the hand when he came forward to see what the trouble was. But now bad luck appeared in the form of a passenger, Deputy US Marshal Horace Loomis.

Loomis knew something was wrong up front, and so he loaded his shotgun and stepped quietly out into the night. Without ceremony the officer dropped Cole Young. The rest of the gang galloped off into the night without their loot.

The gang went on with their small-time robberies, holding up a couple of stages and a series of isolated stores. As usual, their labors produced only pittances of money, plus bits and pieces of liquor and tobacco. There was a good deal of casual brutality connected with these robberies: Bob Hayes pistol-whipped one elderly country postmaster, for example, because he objected to giving up $5.50, all the money he had.

After sticking up another isolated little store, they ran into a posse at the Diamond A horse camp. When Black Jack and Bob Hayes rode into camp, all unsuspecting, the posse blew Hayes off his horse, quite dead. Black Jack got away, even though his horse was killed.

Veteran lawman Jeff Milton and other hunters could not close with the gang. Meanwhile, Black Jack's own paranoia moved him to kill an outlaw, Red Sanders, who he guessed had talked to the law. He then hid out in a tangled, wild canyon ravine, to this day called Black Jack Canyon.

Deputy Marshal Hall, formidable sheriff Fred Higgins, and posse men Bill Hart, Crook-Neck Johnson, and Charlie Paxton set up an ambush in Cole Creek Canyon, down in Graham County. Ironically, it was a lost hat that put paid to Black Jack's career. The lawmen had already folded up their trailside ambush when Higgins turned back to look for his hat. At this moment the posse saw three men on the trail behind them, already reaching for their weapons. The three bandits broke for safety in the thick vegetation, but the posse saw one of them stagger before he could reach cover. He vanished into the vegetation, but the officers decided they had not lost anything in that heavy brush and prudently withdrew.

Later that day a cowboy on the same trail found a mortally wounded Bill Christian. A Mormon freighter then brought into town all that remained of the bandit, tossed on top of a load of lumber. All sorts of people identified the body, although several called him Black Jack Ketchum.

The two bandits who got away were veteran outlaws George Musgrave and Bob Christian. Christian surfaced in Mexico in the autumn of 1897, then dropped out of sight forever. Musgrave retired to South America, dying in 1947.

One curious postscript remains: Black Jack Ketchum, mistaken for Black Jack Christian more than once, made an intriguing comment the day he was to be hanged. He knew Black Jack Christian, he said, and Christian was still alive. "Oh yes," said Ketchum, "I have an idea where he is but I won't tell." And he didn't. The secret, if there was one, went to the grave with Ketchum—both parts of him, for the shock of the drop parted him from his head, and he was buried in two pieces.

With the drop of Ketchum ended the bloody history of the Casey and Christian boys of Oklahoma, their brutality and their nickel-and-dime robberies. They started with nothing and finished the same way, as failures.

Unless you consider the tally of the dead.

Outlaw Heaven

Despite the tiny populations, the saloons of No Man's Land were cesspits of sin and trouble. All manner of ugly things happened in them, like the night long-haired Dick Davis arrived from Tascosa with a couple of dance-hall queens. Dick took his stand at the bar to regale everybody with tales of his own magnificence. His bombast wore very thin very quickly until at last somebody shouted "shoot the jaw," or something like that and, well, somebody did.

A .45 slug broke Dick's jawbone into dozens of pieces and blew out all his teeth but one. Dick collapsed. A local doctor picked out all the fragments he could find, about seventy of them, and Dick survived to carry on a distinguished career as a claim jumper and horse thief.

The law didn't care about Dick getting shot, of course, because there wasn't any law. Criminals simply went unpunished, unless an irate citizenry could organize in time to deal with them. One agonized parent, petitioning the US Department of Justice, bitterly alleged "my boy was killed in June, 1886, at Neutral City" and then went on to list seven more men killed and three badly wounded between that time and February of 1887.

In the early days of white settlement, the panhandle of far-western Oklahoma was a unique place: a brutal, unforgiving land, long the preserve of the Comanche. In the depths of winter, murderous blizzards howled down out of Kansas and Colorado to freeze men and animals while settlers huddled over cattle-chip fires in their isolated sod shanties. For the rest of the year, the winds ranged all the way from gentle breezes to shrieking gales that drove great clouds of dust before them.

For all the growing pains, by the end of 1885, settlement was well advanced, especially along the creeks flowing into the Beaver River. Many settlers lived from hand to mouth and earned what ready cash they could by collecting bones from thousands of carcasses, remains of the great hunts and the bitter blizzards.

As many as fifty to one hundred buffalo skeletons could be found within a few hundred yards. Mingled with them were acres of beef bones, a legacy from the terrible blizzard of 1886. A ton of bones brought $8 to $10 in Dodge City, and horns brought even more, because they were a favorite material for knife handles. Many a poor nester bought crucial groceries by harvesting bones and driving the long haul to Dodge.

Men called it No Man's Land with good reason, for it was not only wild and sparsely settled but lawless in the literal sense of the word. The *New York Sun* called it "God's Land, But No Man's."

The Santa Fe Trail went through No Man's Land, leading up from old Santa Fe into Kansas and the railhead towns. In the nineteenth century it had no government at all. It formed a long, narrow rectangle, altogether about 5,700 square miles. Once it was made up of three massive Spanish land grants and part of the Mexican province of Texas. When the United States annexed Texas, this northern strip was cut off to comply with the slave state part of the "part slave, part free" balance mandated by the Missouri Compromise.

After passage of the 1862 Homestead Act, No Man's Land was surveyed and laid out into townships marked with little domes of zinc, called pot lines. Kansas newspapers published rhapsodic stories of new towns and free land; the embryo town of Beaver would be called the new metropolis of the plains. This paradise sounded wonderful to land-hungry pilgrims, but the land was little more than sage and windswept plains.

There being no law, No Man's Land attracted all kinds of riffraff. The *New York Sun* reporter described one little town's "floating population."

Floating is scarcely the word to describe the population temporarily there. . . . If they floated it was on a sea of alcohol. If they sailed or flew the breeze that wafted them was heavy with the fumes of tobacco and the smoke of gunpowder. If they drifted they were stranded at the shortest of intervals on bars not built of sand.

There were a few other settlements, merely wide spots in the road. Gate City boasted two stores, a blacksmith shop, and a post office. Neutral City was about the same size, except for a bumper crop of saloons, and so was Old Hardesty. Many "cities" consisted of little more than a post office.

Then there was a woebegone settlement called Old Sod Town, a refuse-littered dump of about a dozen sod buildings. Old Sod Town was soon known as the center of operations for an outfit of horse thieves, the Chitwood Gang, who stole anything with four legs until a citizen blew a hole in one of the gang and vigilantes ran the others out of the territory.

Neutral City introduced one young teamster to No Man's Land. Stopped in front of Bly's general store after his long trip, the young man's oxen promptly lay down, and the youngster himself was half asleep. Abruptly Bly emerged from his emporium, brandishing two shotguns and shouting, "Drive that team up a little! Drive that team up!" And before the teamster could get his tired team on its feet and out of the way, Bly was blazing away across the street, from behind a barricade made from slabs of salt meat.

The storekeeper's target was a cowboy called Boone, who was preparing to open a saloon across the street, an undertaking to which Bly objected. Boone, unpersuaded, returned the fire with his Winchester, while the teamster hugged the earth and wondered why he'd come to this benighted place. About a hundred rounds later, as the teamster told it, what passed for silence returned to Neutral City and nobody was hurt.

Along with the hardworking nesters and cattlemen, large and small, came the grifters, the bullies, the killers, and the thieves. In the northeast corner of the strip, a couple of counterfeiters turned out bags of phony coins, most of which they circulated up in Kansas. If the Kansas law got too close, it was easy enough to reach sanctuary down in No Man's Land, where the writ of Kansas law did not apply.

Because No Man's Land belonged to no government, there could be no law enforcement save what the people managed for themselves. In 1885 the US Supreme Court ruled that the area was not part of the Cherokee Outlet to the east, as many had thought. The secretary of the interior opined only that the area was public domain, and therefore open to anybody to settle. And so the citizens handled their own law enforcement, either personally or by forming vigilante groups.

In Beaver City, for example, when a drunk started to shoot up the town, endangering the families there, the citizens simply filled the offender full of holes and buried him without particular ceremony. There was no formal inquest, both because there was no authority to hold one and because nobody cared.

People felt the same way about the case of one Broadhurst, a settler whose wife was insulted by a neighbor. Once he heard of his neighbor's transgression, Broadhurst saddled up, rode to his neighbor's house, and shot him down. His fellow citizens thought some formal gesture ought to be made, so they convened a homegrown court, presided over by a man who had once been a judge somewhere else. The verdict, predictably, was not guilty.

The same maxim disposed of a hoodlum saloon keeper who took umbrage at the town's opposition to his watering hole and passed his time taking potshots at the sod houses of those who opposed him. A storm of return fire extinguished him permanently, and an ad hoc court promptly exonerated the shooter.

The same rough justice was applied to a small group of men organized to jump as many claims as possible. Two of the gang came in second in a gunfight with a hundred or more citizens, who then loaded the surviving families of the miscreants into their wagons, complete with all their belongings, and sent them on their way. Justice was done again in No Man's Land.

To settle disputed land titles, some of the strip's leading citizens created the Respective Claims Board. The board adjudicated disputed land titles and abated the nuisance of the "road trotters," a group of roadside thieves. The board's authority depended mostly on the rifles of its own members, and in most cases that power sufficed.

It worked perfectly with another gang of road trotters who got their comeuppance in Beaver in 1887. The worst of the bunch, one Thompson, had already tried to kill the locally elected marshal, Addison Mundell, and now was ordered by the Respective Claims Board to vacate a disputed claim. When

Thompson arrogantly refused, Mundell and a posse set out for his dugout on the claim.

Spotting them from a boardinghouse window, Thompson shouted and raised his rifle. Mundell was quicker, however, and put a bullet through Thompson's knee. Taking Thompson to his dugout, where the local sawbones amputated his ravaged leg, the posse now searched for his confederates, Tracy and Bennett. Tracy wisely departed the area at a high lope, but Bennett stuck around too long and was apprehended and led to the dugout. As he faced his wounded cohort, the last sound he heard on earth was the cocking of many hammers. Bennett departed this life forthwith, and the posse immediately sent Thompson to join him. The matter was then closed with an ad hoc coroner's inquest, which opined as follows: "We the jury appointed to view the remains . . . find that they came to their death from gunshot wounds received at the hands of many law-abiding citizens, there inflicting, as nearly as possible, the extreme penalty of the law as it should be in such cases. . . . [T]heir untimely end is but the result of their many wrongs."

A couple of locals opined that Mundell had dry-gulched Thompson, but the jury either didn't believe them or didn't care or both. It was sufficient to be rid of this arrogant pest.

Bennett and Thompson were not the only iniquitous residents to be cut off in their own wickedness. A hoodlum called Billy Olive shot up a saloon in Beaver, working on the false premise that Henderson, the bartender, had induced Olive's lady's departure from the saloon. Olive and a partner, "Lengthy" Halford, pursued the bartender out the saloon door and into the street. Escaping when Olive's rifle misfired, Henderson lay in wait for his tormentor behind a sod wall and drilled him dead center. Lengthy wisely departed in haste for safer climes, and public opinion exonerated Henderson without a hearing of any kind.

And then there was the celebrated case of Doc Linley's hat. Linley was a shady sort with more than one wife, but he was a sartorial triumph, regularly sporting a Prince Albert coat and a shiny top hat. Of an evening in a saloon, a man called Brusher placed Doc's fine hat on his own head. "Let me see how I will look with that thing on," he said. And he looked wonderful indeed, or at least he did until Clark, another celebrant, decided to demonstrate his keen eye by shooting the hat off Brusher's head. Being somewhat pie-eyed, Clark sadly shot a trifle low, puncturing Brusher's forehead instead of the hat.

The town mayor, all the law there was, fined Clark $25 for criminal carelessness in handling his pistol. And that was an end to the matter, or it was until Brusher's brother came to town. After hearing the evidence, the brother graciously announced that his sibling's death was clearly accidental and even had a drink with Clark. One drink followed another, merry as a wedding bell, until Brusher politely excused himself, went outside, then stuck his pistol through the saloon window, and permanently ventilated Clark.

Similar rough justice pursued a No Man's Land hoodlum called Bill Bridgford. Riding along a road one day, Bridgford, from either malice or a warped sense of sport, fired a couple of shots over the head of a woman and her child traveling behind him in her buggy. The lady's vehicle upset, and she fled in terror with her child, much to Bridgford's amusement.

He shouldn't have laughed. That night in Neutral City, retribution came looking for Bridgford, in the person of the local vigilance committee. As Bridgford partook of strong spirits in a local saloon, the local enforcers summoned him to come forth and answer for his mistreatment of a lady. This failing, "some parties on the outside opened fire on the house, firing through the side on which there were no windows, thus placing the parties on the inside at a disadvantage."

No doubt. Bridgford was mortally wounded, an innocent cowboy patron got a slug in the arm, and Rockhold, the bartender, was hit twice. Boone, one of Bridgford's disreputable partners, outside on the other side of the saloon, took flight and galloped into a barbed-wire fence, killing his horse and badly cutting himself.

The vigilantes burned down the offending saloon, then ordered the surviving occupants of the bar to leave town, on the general grounds of being found in noxious company. All obeyed but Rockhold, who not only hung around but jumped another man's claim. When his victim objected, Rockhold shot him, and that night the vigilantes saddled up again. They surrounded Rockhold's soddy, but the bartender refused to emerge and killed one citizen who had just finished pouring kerosene on the building. In the ensuing fire and confusion, Rockhold escaped with only minor wounds and was never brought to justice this side of the pearly gates.

In time most of the bad men went the way of Rockhold or Bridgford: dead or fled. One pair, who incautiously bragged that they intended to rob the big distillery on Hog Creek, were hanged by a vigilance committee before they could commit their crime, a sort of preventive medicine. Others were dealt with summarily by people they tried to bully—to the satisfaction of the general citizenry.

222

222222222

Thus ended Bill Williams, the Bad Man of Gate City. Bill had won a measure of dubious fame when he emerged from his shack, drunk, forgetting he had tied his half-broken horse to the building. As Bill tried to gallop off into the sunset, his horse remained attached to the shack and went berserk, the shack disintegrated, and Bill ended up south-end-first in a prickly pear.

Bill's disaster called for urgent surgery of the roughest frontier kind. Bill was stretched facedown on the saloon bar while the spines of the prickly pear were extracted from his posterior one by one. Bill swore horribly throughout the procedure, the citizens doing the job pulling slowly, pretending a desire not to hurt him.

Having drunk up most of the town, and perhaps still smarting from prickly pear, Bill entertained himself on his departure by firing over the heads of an inoffensive man and woman chopping wood. Just watch how fast settlers can run, Bill said to a companion, and the terrified couple did indeed run.

The man ran, however, even faster than Bill thought possible. In fact, he ran to collect his shotgun and cut through his cornfield to confront the Bad Man of Gate City farther down the trail. Astonished at finding his late victim armed and angry, Bill reached for his pistol. He was too slow.

For a while a big-time criminal or two operated in No Man's Land. Black Jack Ketchum, the story goes, three times held up the railroad over in New Mexico and twice fled to the safety of a ranch in No Man's Land. He and his men escaped unscathed, but a third holdup was a mistake. Because this time the conductor badly maimed Black Jack's arm with a load of buckshot. The engineer paid his respects to the conductor: "You said you were tired of having your train robbed. Now I believe you."

In addition to the general run of no-goods, No Man's Land was amply supplied with liquor sellers and brothels. There were a good many of the former, thanks in large measure to ax-wielding Carrie Nation and her Anti-Saloon League. Carrie's crusades up in Kansas pretty well dried up the Sunflower State, and the nearest place for Kansans to get a legal drink was No Man's Land.

Liberal, just across the Kansas line, was an especially thirsty town. The Rock Island railhead reached Liberal in the spring of 1888, a stockyard appeared, and the cattlemen and cowboys followed. These men were given to celebrating in style, and to accommodate their taste for booze and other more intimate indoor sports, a little town popped up just over the border in No Man's Land, like a mushroom after rain. It called itself Beer City.

Early on, Beer City bore the more respectable name of White City, because it was roofed mostly in canvas, but Beer City was obviously a more appropriate title, and the name stuck. There was nothing much in Beer City but saloons and dance halls. Its business was exclusively women and booze, its only customers, men with a prodigious appetite for both.

The town had other kinds of entertainment, too, much of it unplanned and violent. There was, for example, the day on which Pussy Cat Nell, madam of the house above the Yellow Snake Saloon, ushered town marshal Lew Bush into the next world with her shotgun. The cause of their falling out is not recorded, but there is no evidence that Pussy Cat Nell's impulsive act was regarded as worthy of censure. Besides, she ran an essential service, and Lew doubled in rustling on the side.

Because Beer City and its competitors were a very long way from any kind of real distillery, and because cowboys seldom cared much about what sort of booze they drank, the liquor supply, such as it was, tended to come from local sources. Thus the making of white lightning became a favorite—and semirespectable—occupation for a good many residents of No Man's Land.

In addition to innumerable little stills producing more or less poisonous rotgut, there were several serious distilleries. One was run out of a cave covered by a lean-to soddy on Hog Creek, near Gate City, and it ran night and day. Another, down on the Clearwater River south of Beaver, produced a couple of barrels of "good" whiskey each week. The best-known still even boasted an expert distiller, imported all the way from Kentucky. Another artist boiled dried peaches and added the juice to his moonshine, producing an amber-colored and fancy-flavored drink.

No Man's Land's best-known hoodlum was Bill Coe, who called himself Captain Coe and Bud Coe. He acquired an equally worthless following and ensconced himself in an inhospitable area called Black Mesa, a rugged, rocky plateau that spreads across parts of three states, including northwest Oklahoma. Its highest point reaches almost five thousand feet, and it made an ideal refuge for an outlaw gang.

Sometime in the 1860s, Coe found a lair near Lookout Point, from which his gang set about robbing people on the Santa Fe Trail. The gang grew, expanding from perhaps fifteen felons to as many as fifty. On Black Mesa they built themselves a combination fortress-house with stone walls, windowless but with copious loopholes for defense. Two big fireplaces kept the building warm and the place was complete with a bar and a piano.

In 1867 Coe was throwing an even wider loop, striking the larger ranchers. In February of that year, they raided the big sheep ranch of the Bernal brothers, making off with more than three thousand head and killing three of the Bernals' men. The army caught and hanged eleven of Coe's men out of hand and used artillery to shell the stone house into junk. Coe ran for it but was chased throughout New Mexico and Colorado, where he left this earth care of a rope and a tall tree.

In time the plague of outlaws abated to some degree, and enthusiastic residents of No Man's Land formed a provisional government, as they called it. They even had a "great seal" made and put it on petitions to Washington in a bid to obtain territorial status. They grandly called their new land Cimarron Territory, in the forlorn hope that the name and their activity would move the Congress to favorably consider their ambitions. They sent representatives to Washington, too, and even found some allies in Congress, but the strip remained an orphan.

It remained so until it was attached to the brand-new Oklahoma Territory by the 1890 Organic Act. But with the price of wheat low and a massive drought in 1888, No Man's Land lost much of what population remained.

Soon many of the criminals also drifted away, because few people had any money. Even the provisional government folded up. And when the Oklahoma lands to the east opened for settlement in 1889, many people pulled up stakes and went to join the rush.

The population dropped swiftly from about twelve thousand to under three thousand, and as one old-timer opined, the citizens had to include some prairie dogs and jack rabbits to get that number.

The Undistinguished Career of Bill Dalton

Surly Amateur

Bill Dalton's henchman turned his Winchester on Longview City's Marshal Matt Muckleroy and blasted him in the belly. Muckleroy was fortunate, however, for the round caromed off some silver dollars the lawman carried in a pouch in his pocket, split, and did no permanent damage. He eventually recovered from his wound. More serious was the wound of a saloon keeper, J. W. McQueen, hit as he ran into the alley at the beginning of the firefight. The shot that slammed into McQueen's body seemed for a while to be a mortal wound, but he too eventually recovered.

Another citizen, Charles Leonard, who was merely walking through the "court house yard," was hit in the left hand. Other accounts say that mill hand Charlie Learn—presumably the same man—was murdered near the courthouse fence. Bill Dalton had finally realized his dream of being a real bandit leader. It wouldn't last long.

There are myriad tales about Bill Dalton, probably as many as there are about his more infamous brothers. He came from California, where he lived at a place he called a ranch outside Paso Robles. Born in Missouri in 1865, he married in California and fathered a couple of children.

Bill Dalton, looking unusually pensive *Western History Collections, University of Oklahoma Libraries*

All kinds of wonderful myths surround his life there, including tales that he was wealthy, that he served in the legislature, that he fathered a child out of wedlock down in Hugo, Oklahoma, and that he had a covey of mistresses. All of these are false except the possibility that he may have been wealthy. Even so, he certainly detested what he considered the "Establishment," especially the Southern Pacific Railroad, which many farmers believed was corrupt and oppressive in its dealings with ordinary people.

Dalton also had a real talent for resurrection, mostly at the hands of newspapers. At various times during his relatively short outlaw season, the public read about his demise. In late summer of 1893, he apparently died at Ingalls. Rising from the grave, he was killed at Sacred Heart Mission in the spring of 1894. A whole regiment of lawmen shot him yet again before he was well and truly extinguished in the summer of 1894. Though by now he was buried in California, he revived and was captured in New York in 1896. One book even concluded that he committed suicide in Wyoming.

But most of Dalton's carnage took place in Oklahoma. At first he joined up with veteran outlaw Bill Doolin, who had rallied a new gaggle of outlaws assembled from survivors of the old Dalton aggregation. The Doolin Gang, as the new group was called, promptly became a thorn in the side of honest men. It grew, according to some estimates, to as many as twelve or fourteen men.

In the wild 1893 shootout with the Doolin Gang in the outlaw town of Ingalls, Oklahoma Territory, three deputy US marshals were killed. All but one of the gang members galloped to safety and went on with their nefarious doings, although

Arkansas Tom Jones (aka Roy Daugherty) was captured during the Ingalls fight and sent to prison.

The papers deluged their readers with the usual flood of misinformation, including the news that Dalton had killed Lafe Shadley, one of the lawmen. In fact, it appears that Shadley and the other two lawmen were killed by Arkansas Tom, sniping from his room at a hotel. Various reports had Dalton shot once or maybe twice, along with Bitter Creek Newcomb and somebody called Dynamite Bill. Dalton was portrayed as the leader of the gang.

While the gang lasted, they were a terror. On January 23, 1894, for example, Doolin and Tulsa Jack Blake, backed up by Bitter Creek Newcomb, struck the Farmers' and Merchants' Bank of Pawnee, Oklahoma Territory. They got only $300 on this raid because the bank's time lock was still set, but they temporarily kidnapped the cashier, releasing him only when they were well clear of the town.

Less than two months later, Doolin and Bill Dalton, with other gang members waiting outside town, kidnapped the station agent at Woodward in the wee hours, took him to the station, and forced him to open the Santa Fe safe. They got away with some $6,500 on this raid, a considerable sum for the time.

In the aftermath of the Woodward robbery, lawmen circulated a detailed description of Bill Dalton: "Twenty five years old, five feet ten inches tall, weight 170 pounds, two weeks growth of beard, slouch hat with high crown and crease in top, pants in boots, checkered handkerchief about his neck, dark suit, sack coat, dark complexion."

The depredations of the Doolin Gang at last inspired Chief Justice Frank Dale of the Territorial Supreme Court to call in

Marshal Evett Dumas Nix and issue some famous instructions, practical if somewhat unjudicial.

"Marshal," said Judge Dale, "I have reached the conclusion that the only good outlaw is a dead one. I hope you will instruct your deputies in the future to bring them in dead." The gang's days were numbered.

During a robbery of a store at tiny Sacred Heart, Bill Dalton and Bitter Creek Newcomb shot down a tough elderly shopkeeper who strongly objected to being robbed by couple of hoodlums. In return the old man put a bullet into Bitter Creek. It was after Sacred Heart that Doolin and Dalton parted ways. The reason they rode their separate ways may have been Dalton's ambition to lead his own gang, or maybe it was the intelligent Doolin's conviction that Dalton was too much of a loose cannon to ride with any longer.

On his own Dalton decided to recruit some guns to help him and try his wings as an independent operator. He started with bank robbery. Although Dalton had a world of arrogant self-confidence and an overactive mouth to go with it, it does not appear that he ever amounted to much as an outlaw leader.

Still, Bill Dalton's name was well known, and a bewildering collection of newspaper stories reported him and his gang in a variety of places as far apart as Wagoner, Oklahoma Territory; Kendallville, Indiana; and Washington, DC. According to the *Cherokee Advocate*, they had "over fifty murders to their credit."

Bill Dalton left his wife and children at a farm owned by Houston Wallace. It was a shabby place near the little town of Elk, down in the neighborhood of the city of Andmore, Oklahoma. Now an independent operator, Dalton turned his attention to Texas, where he had not been reported as visiting so far. The target was the First National Bank of Longview, located in that little town in the eastern part of the state. Dalton put together a collection of unimpressive bad men, including Jim Wallace, brother of Houston Wallace. Jim Wallace took the "nom de robber" of George Bennett.

To Wallace, Dalton added a couple of other eager criminals, usually identified as the two Knight (possibly Nite) brothers, Jim and Big Asa. Other sources reported that the other outlaws were local sawmill hands Jim Jones and Will Jones. Or maybe one of them was George Bennett, or perhaps Tom Littleton, or even Charles White.

These additional amateur hard cases, whoever they were, would give Dalton his very own gang. This dubious aggregation was a very far cry from the Daltons of other days, or the old, bold James-Younger Gang, but ever-cocky Bill Dalton must have figured his new confederates ought to suffice to knock over a little country bank.

Dalton simply did a reconnaissance of the town alone— maybe doing some solitary fishing in the Sabine River or maybe, as other sources say, wetting a line with the rest of his gang. Now the gang was ready to seize their jackpot. One or two stayed with the all-important horses in an alley behind the First National; Dalton and the fourth man went inside. Dalton had ready a curious note, written in pencil on the back of a poster; he handed it to the cashier, Tom Clemmons:

> Home, May 23
> The First National Bank, Longview
> This will introduce to you Charles Speckelmeyer, who
> wants some money and is going to have it. B and F.

Clemmons did not take the note seriously. He thought it was some sort of charity appeal and was ready to donate something. But then he found himself looking down the muzzle of Dalton's Winchester and realized he had big trouble. While Dalton held Clemmons and other bankmen at gunpoint, another robber, probably Big Asa, pushed through a door behind the counter area and quickly scooped up whatever money he could find. The haul included, as the *Daily Oklahoman* reported, "$2000 in ten-dollar bills numbered 9, and nine $20 bills numbered 20, and a quantity of unsigned bank notes."

A bank officer scuffled briefly with one of the bandits, and everyone else in the bank intelligently took this opportunity to run out the back door and disappear. The outlaws herded Tom Clemmons and his brother J. R. in front of them out of the bank.

Bill Dalton's plans began to unravel when the local law spotted his gang outside the Longview bank and grew suspicious. Or maybe, as the *Longview Morning Journal* later reported, the alarm might have been given by a businessman, John Welborne. It seems one of the bandits had invited him in, but Welborne wasn't having any part of all those guns. He ran off down the street shouting that the bank was being robbed.

However the word passed around the town, armed citizens converged from all directions, and a wild firefight broke out in the alley. The outlaws inside the bank cleared out in a hurry. They tried to drive the bank employees with them toward their horses, using them as human shields, but their hostages were having none of this and ran away in another direction.

The shooting in the alley rose to a roar as the outlaws traded shots with an assortment of angry citizens and peace officers. George Buckingham, a bartender, grabbed a pistol and ran to the sound of the guns; he was one of the first citizens on the scene, and his reward was a slug in the face from Wallace's rifle. Buckingham died before he could fire a shot.

By all accounts Wallace was shooting a saddle gun from the hip and was, as citizen P. T. Boyd said much later, "a dead shot with his Winchester Special." The weapon was afterward found to have sights made of bone. "The story," said a later president of the bank, "and I don't doubt the truth of it, is that the piece of bone is from a human skull; from the head of one of Bennett's [Wallace's] victims."

Wallace seemed to be doing most of the shooting, and most of the damage, but he was running out of luck. After city marshal Muckleroy went down, his deputy, Will Stevens, stood his ground in a shower of outlaw bullets and got a round into Wallace. Or maybe, according to another citizen, the fatal round came from a hardware merchant, who in later years refused to be identified by the press.

[He s]tuck his single-action Colt .45 through an open window of a near-by brick building. He leveled down on Bennett [Wallace] just as the desperado turned to drop City Marshal Muckelroy. . . . [T]he man with the .45 wouldn't shoot until Bennett [Wallace] turned again to face him. The bandit saw that menacing Colt as he turned and both of the men fired at about the same time.

The unidentified merchant is quoted as saying, perhaps a trifle pompously, that he "could have gotten Bill Dalton and one of the Nite boys from my place in the window . . . but they had their backs turned . . . and I wouldn't shoot even a murdering bank robber in the back." But later newspaper accounts of the fight state that Wallace was shot in the back, and it's hard to imagine any Westerner having such scruples in the midst of a firefight in which his fellow citizens were being shot.

Or maybe the shooter was somebody else altogether. Local attorney Claude Lacy got credit for the shooting, said a retired city judge:

> Claude was in the saloon next to the bank when the shooting started and he ran to the door. . . .[O]ne of Bennett's [Wallace's] bullets shattered the glass in the door and forced him to run in the other direction, into a feed store. . . . [T]he windows at the back of the store looked out on the alley and Claude got behind some sacks of feed and drilled Bennett in the back. . . . At least, he always got credit for shooting him first but the man was hit from all directions.

Whoever fired the fatal round, or rounds, Wallace went down, dying, and the rest of the gang took to their heels.

Across the Oklahoma line lawmen recovered the outlaws' horses, the animals exhausted from being pushed too hard. However, Dalton and his two remaining cronies stole more horses near Stringtown and turned west toward the Muddy Boggy, riding into the Chickasaw Nation. And there, on May 29, the trail apparently ended.

But the officers did not stop looking. They were as sick of arrogant outlaws as Judge Dale was, and the Longview bank had offered a $500 reward for the robbers. The Longview citizenry had chipped in another $200, making a tidy reward for lawmen accustomed to facing great danger for miserable pay. There were various newspaper reports that members of the gang had been captured, none of which were accurate. But at last, in early June, the patient officers got a break.

In Ardmore the perennially impoverished Houston Wallace bought provisions, including ammunition, to the tune of some $200. The store owner, uneasy at such unusual purchases by Wallace, took the bills to the US commissioner. He wired Longview and quickly learned that the $10 bills were part of the loot from the bank robbery. Wallace may have bought a wagon as well, which would have further aroused suspicion.

Deputy US Marshal Seldon Lindsey followed Wallace to the express office. There, accompanied by two women who kept their sunbonnets pulled close around their faces, Wallace presented a package pickup order. The express agent produced the package, but Wallace refused to sign a receipt for it. Lindsey then arrested all three on suspicion of introducing liquor into Indian Territory—a federal offense—and the box was broken open forthwith. Sure enough, it contained nine quarts of red-eye.

Wallace caved in quickly. "The whiskey is not mine," he said. "It's for some people who are staying with me." The women would not say much at all, beyond giving the unenlightening names of Smith and Pruitt. They even refused to say where they lived, but Lindsey drew his own conclusions. Wallace was forthwith consigned to the local jail, and the two women were placed under guard.

The deputy marshal headed for Wallace's farm. Six other deputy US marshals rode out in two groups, joined by two local officers, and they surrounded the place, which was a two-room shanty. The lawmen took their places early in the morning on June 8.

As the officers encircled the Wallace farmhouse, Deputy US Marshal Loss Hart worked his way toward a ravine in back of the house. The ravine provided the only obvious escape route, because it was the only path away from the shack that had any useful cover. Before Hart could get all the way to the ravine, a man emerged onto the house porch, saw Lindsey, and dashed back inside. He immediately reappeared, jumping out of a back window, and this time he had a pistol in his hand. As he sprinted for the deep ravine that would give him cover, Hart shouted at him to halt, but the man turned and raised his pistol to shoot at the lawman. Oklahoma City's *Daily Oklahoman* put it well, albeit a little dramatically:

> A .44 ball, hot from the deputy's Winchester, tore into his body at the waistband near the right rear suspender button, and with two convulsive leaps he fell.
>
> Bill Dalton, the notorious desperado and bandit, met his death on the 8th inst. at Elk, I. T. C. L. Hart, a deputy marshal of the Paris district, fired the shot that sent the spirit of the outlaw to its home. . . . Hart . . . called on him to halt. Dalton half turned around, tried to take aim while running, and just then the officer shot. Two jumps in the air were the only motions made.

The *Fort Worth Gazette* reported Dalton went down before the "unerring aim" of Loss Hart, "[a] .44 Winchester hole at the pants band on the right side of the spinal column, near the hip, shows where the little messenger of justice had rid the country of the worst outlaw who ever stole a horse or shot a man in the Southwest."

Inside the tiny house the officers found six terrified children, and bolts of silk cloth stuffed with numerous crisp bills and a Longview bank sack. A couple of the children told the officers their names were Dalton. After an initial denial of any relation to Dalton, one of the two women arrested in Ardmore the day before at last broke down when she saw Dalton's body. She then confirmed she was Bill Dalton's wife.

Although poor Adeline Dalton had still another sorrow to bear, most people rejoiced at Dalton's passage. As did the *Daily Oklahoman:* "Stretched out on a pine board in the rooms of Undertaker Appolis on Caddo street . . . Bill Dalton . . . lies stiff and cold . . . a .44 Winchester hole at the pants band on the right side of the spinal column . . . and that small piece of lead has rid the country of the worst outlaw who ever stole a horse or shot a man."

From a photograph Houston Wallace identified his brother as the bandit deputy Stevens killed at Longview. There was no trace of the Knight brothers at Ardmore. They had evaded pursuit this time, but they were headed for the same bitter end that awaited every man who rode with the Doolin-Dalton outfit. It took more than a year for fate to catch up with the Knights, but at last the two brothers—and a criminal cohort, Jim Crane—were run down and killed on the Charles Schneider ranch along Bear Creek in Menard County, Texas.

What remained of Bill Dalton was shipped off to sunny California, where it was duly planted in Merced County. A newspaper story from Ardmore reported the departure under a heading that solemnly announced, MR. DALTON CONTINUES DEAD. AND AMAZINGLY, TO THE EDITORIAL DISGUST OF VARIOUS NEWSPAPERS. "[A] burning shame," said the *Daily Ardmorite*. A federal grand jury much later indicted Loss Hart and the rest of the lawmen with him for the murder of Dalton, "the worst outlaw ever to . . . shoot a man." The officers were released on their own recognizance, and there is no record that they were ever tried.

So perished the last of the outlaw Daltons, joining the long line of Oklahoma hoodlums killed by peace officers. And others were still to die under the guns of the law. Of the several members of the Dalton-Doolin Gangs, the swaggering hard cases with the jaunty nicknames and the larger-than-life reputations, just one outlaw—aside from Emmett Dalton—died of natural causes. This man, Little Bill Raidler, debilitated by his old gunshot wounds, did not long survive his release from prison. The last man to go was Arkansas Tom Jones (aka Roy Daugherty) in 1924, back in the robbing business after stretches in prison and even a spell of honest employment. With his death in Joplin, Missouri, thoroughly ventilated by lawmen's bullets, passed the last of the old gang.

It is not recorded that there was any widespread mourning.

Bob Rogers
Psychopath

Jess Elliot was a lawyer and Cherokee constable, and he was in Catoosa to serve legal papers. He ended up in a Catoosa saloon, and there he met Bob Rogers. Both men had been drinking, and they soon locked horns.

Their falling-out soon escalated into a fistfight, which Rogers clearly won. With Elliot on the saloon floor, other men stopped the fight. Rogers left, and Elliot was persuaded to stay in the bar and recuperate until he could ride. Elliot rested up a little, then went outside, mounted, and rode off.

He did not get far, because Rogers was lying in wait for him. Rogers charged into the constable and knocked him out of the saddle, then dismounted and drew his knife. Rogers cut Elliot's throat, making three horrible gashes, and left him in the roadway.

Elliot bled to death in less than half an hour, as other men, including a doctor, tried to save him. When Elliot died, they stayed with the body, building a fire and sending one of their number to fetch Deputy Marshal John Taylor. But before Taylor could reach them, Rogers suddenly appeared out of the night. While the horrified townsmen looked on, Rogers rode through the fire, ran off the doctor and the other men, and then kicked and stomped the lifeless body of his victim, rummaged through Elliot's papers, and rode off into the gloom.

Marshal Taylor trailed Rogers as far as Sapulpa, but there the trail went cold. After his ghastly outrage against Elliot, nobody could doubt that Rogers had a crazy streak, or that he would ride on to other devilment.

Rogers's career outside the law started in a small way with horse theft. He lifted about a dozen of somebody else's animals in the territory, drove his booty over into Arkansas, and sold them. Deputy Marshal Heck Bruner didn't have to spend much time pursuing Rogers before he duly dragged him back to Fort Smith to face the formidable federal judge, Isaac Parker.

Because of Rogers's youth—he was nineteen the first time he met Parker—Parker decided to be lenient in this, Rogers's first offense. He gave the young man a prison sentence, but suspended it and put Rogers on probation.

During his customary sentencing lecture, Parker gave Rogers some good advice, as he often did with badmen who appeared before him. "This is your first offense, lad," the judge said kindly. "If you continue in this path of life, death may be the penalty." It was very good counsel indeed, but Rogers paid no attention to it at all and quickly returned to his burgeoning career of larceny. In the fall of 1891, he was charged with assault with intent to kill a lawman but released on bond.

He was not tried for this offense and for a time he remained near Catoosa where he met Jess Elliot. As sure as sunrise, after the Elliot murder Rogers returned, and he had put together his own little gang, a collection of scum nearly as bad as he was. Two of them were the brothers Kiowa and Dynamite Jack Turner, the latter already wanted for murder in Colorado. The other hoodlums were Willis Brown and Bob Stiteler. It is said that the gang struck out to emulate the Daltons, and for a little while their criminal career went reasonably well. In a period of two months in 1893, they managed two successful robberies, one on the Katy railroad line and a second on the Kansas and Arkansas Valley road near the Seminole switch. They also hit a bank at Mound Valley up in Labette County, Kansas.

They had a brief collision in the summer of 1893 with able deputy marshal Heck Bruner and a posse out west of Vinita. Most of the gang managed to escape the ambush, but the lawmen killed Rogers's brother Sam and one Ralph Halleck.

Then, just before Christmas of 1893, they tried a job on a Katy train north of Vinita, but the engineer put the hammer down and dashed through the ambush. Frustrated, the gang opened fire as the train rushed past them, hitting the fireman in the jaw. But their bonanza was long gone.

On the same day, however, they managed to get this business of train robbery right. This time it was an Arkansas Valley train, which the gang successfully diverted onto a siding crowded with freight cars. The boys must have figured that their luck was with them again.

By and large, things had started reasonably well for the gang, in spite of losing men to the relentless Heck Bruner. But Rogers and Stiteler incautiously paid a visit to Rogers's brother-in-law, Henry Daniels. They, in turn, were visited by Deputy Marshal W. C. Smith.

Rogers was warming his feet before Daniels's fire when he looked up to see the bad end of Smith's revolver. The officer sent Rogers's brother-in-law upstairs to bring Stiteler down and Stiteler was forthwith arrested. But before Smith could get his quarry out of the house, Rogers hit him in the head and Stiteler disappeared into the night. The law went a-hunting, and the unfortunate Stiteler was back in custody before daybreak. But

Rogers was long gone to rejoin the remains of his gang. The law pressed on with its search.

In January 1894 Deputy Marshal Heck Bruner led a posse to the gang's overnight camp on Big Creek and a gunfight erupted. Caught by surprise, the gang came in a bad second. Kiowa was killed and Willis Brown was badly wounded, hurt so badly that he would die at Vinita on the return trip to Fort Smith. Dynamite Jack, despite his ferocious name, surrendered. But once again, Rogers disappeared.

Early in 1895 Rogers seems to have tried his hand at running booze into Indian Territory, a federal offense. Warrants were also issued for him on charges of robbing two men, C. W. Adams and William Wiley. Rogers's fortunes had sunk very low by now. At last he ran out of luck altogether, just a week after robbing Wiley.

Rogers had been elusive for a long time, but he chose to stay in his regular stomping grounds rather than ride away. Nor could he avoid the law forever, not with the expert hounds of the marshal service baying on his back trail.

On March 13, 1895, the law finally caught up with Rogers. He was staying overnight with his father near Horseshoe Mound. Ironically, the place was only some twenty miles south of Coffeyville, Kansas, scene of the Dalton Gang's disaster less than three years before. After midnight a large posse led by Deputy Marshal Jim Mayes stashed its horses in a thicket and surrounded the Rogers house. Once his men were in position, Mayes and eight others approached the front of the building.

The elder Rogers appeared on the porch to ask what they wanted, and Mayes told him bluntly, "We want your son. The house is surrounded and he can't escape this time. Light a lamp." Rogers's father had no choice but to follow Mayes's orders, and the posse entered. Their quarry was upstairs. "Come down, Bob," Marshal Mayes called, "and surrender."

The reply was vintage Rogers, "Come and get me."

Three of the lawmen, led by Deputy Marshal W. C. Daniels, went up the stairs to bring Rogers down. Rogers met the three deputies at the head of the stairs. He had a revolver in each hand, but Daniels bravely challenged him. "Drop those guns," he said, and a sane, sensible man probably would have done just that.

But this was Bob Rogers, who apparently was neither sane nor sensible, and he opened fire on the lawmen point-blank. Daniels went down immediately with a bullet through the heart, and a second deputy, Phil Williams, took a serious arm wound. Williams fell backward into the third lawman, and the two tumbled together back down the stairs.

The rest of the lawmen opened a furious fire on the house, driving somewhere between two and three hundred rounds through the board walls of the building. The bombardment continued until the house was riddled with holes and some of the rafters were practically cut in two, but Rogers was still unhurt. The posse then sent the elder Rogers into the house to summon his son to surrender, but Rogers would not listen, even to his father. He defiantly retorted, "I'll give up after I am killed."

Mayes's response was more rifle fire. Rogers remained miraculously unwounded, though his father was said to have been wounded—in the big toe, of all places. But then Rogers called out to the posse men, offering to surrender "if you let me bring my gun."

This dubious offer must have sounded risky to Mayes and his men, but it was better than trying to send anybody back up those deadly stairs. Mayes agreed that Rogers could bring his rifle with him but cautioned the outlaw to keep the muzzle of the weapon pointed down.

The marshal and his men sensibly took cover behind a stack of poles in the yard and waited for Rogers to appear. When their quarry walked out the door, Mayes stood up behind the poles. Rogers stopped and asked a strange question, "Do you have a warrant for me?"

"No," said the marshal, "and [we] don't need one."

Which was perfectly true.

At which Rogers raised the muzzle of the Winchester, but this time he never got off a shot. The whole posse opened up on him as one, and Rogers went down full of holes. He had been hit by twenty-two bullets and two shotgun loads.

So ended the bizarre and brutal career of Bob Rogers.

All of eastern Oklahoma could sleep more soundly.

The Martin Boys
They Died with Their Boots On

Sam Martin was a tobacco-chewing lout of about twenty-four when he took up the outlaw pastime with a bang in May of 1899. His brother Will was about twenty years old, an oaf with a nervous tic on the left side of his face. The immediate cause of their elevation to really serious crime was the law-abiding Hull family.

While the Martins were hurrahing in the town of Mulhall, their gunplay had stampeded Hull's livestock. Hull filed charges against the two but nothing came of it except that he earned the brothers' rancor. And now they stopped Hull and his family on a country road, and their anger at the farmer showed plainly. After he had filed charges against them, they had attempted to take their anger out of Hull's hide, but the big farmer proved too tough for them. But now they were armed to the teeth and Hull was not. And he had his family with him, his little daughter and his pregnant wife.

Hull offered the brothers what little money he had, but they wanted more. Get out of the area in five days or come up with $150, Sam ordered. When the farmer protested that he would have to sell his farm to raise that much, Sam told him that if he didn't do as the brothers ordered, they would dynamite his farm.

Hull didn't have that kind of money, but he tried to borrow it. He didn't have the credit, however, and he followed the banker's advice and went to see the law. He was afraid to sign a

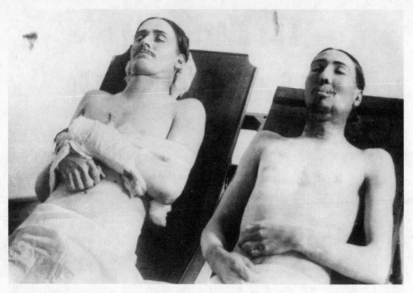

The Martin brothers, extinct
Western History Collections, University of Oklahoma Libraries

complaint, but the local deputy sent three lawmen off to investigate. Hull went along to show them the way to the Martin farm out on Skeleton Creek. The brothers weren't there, a resident said, but they had moved on to another farm, owned by the Simmons family.

When the three deputies arriving at the Simmons place demanded the brothers show their faces, the two ran out the back door and the officers gave chase. The Martins opened up on them, and the officers shot back. One lawman's shots knocked Will down, hit by ten or twelve buckshot, and Sam was seen to stagger as he ran to safety. Will was apprehended and charged, but the grand jury failed to indict.

Recovering from his wounds, Will left Mulhall and rejoined his brother. The two hoodlums were just getting started.

The Martins rode up through No Man's Land and ultimately into little Cimarron, west of Dodge City. Along the way they equipped themselves with a pair of 1895 Winchesters, and Sam got himself an especially handsome Colt with stag horn–handled grips. They held up several little stores and isolated farm families as they worked their way up the Arkansas, and people noticed the beautiful Colt and the two new rifles. If the brothers were trying to conceal their identity, they weren't doing much of a job of it.

They made it back to Oklahoma in March 1903 and invaded the train depot at Hennessey in the Oklahoma Territory. Somebody recognized them and murmured "the Martins," but the outlaws could not identify who had spoken. One of the four men present in the station noted that the smaller of the robbers had a facial tic. That tic would confirm the identity of the bandits.

The robbery didn't pay off in booty. The depot cash drawer had a measly $8.35, and the bandits went to work on the safe, hacking away with a hammer and crowbar and getting nowhere. The robbers tore apart some packages in the freight office. And then they killed a man, a harmless civilian who did not threaten them.

The victim was a young black man named Gus Cravatt, who was minding his own business until somebody across the street in the darkness yelled at him to halt. He thought one of the railroad men was joking, and as he was crossing the railroad track, a rifle bullet tore into his thigh. A night watchman responded to Cravatt's cries, and he was shot at. He returned the fire until his pistol jammed. The outlaws ran then, got to their horses, and galloped off into the gloom.

The watchman and some citizens carried the young man to his father's house, and two doctors did their best for him. They could not stop the gush of blood from a torn artery, however, and Cravatt soon died. When daylight came the next morning, a large, angry posse took up the chase, as the fleeing outlaws repeatedly abandoned exhausted horses and stole other horses and teams. At one point the law got close enough to exchange gunfire with the outlaws, but the pursuers could not bring their quarry to bay.

Near the town of Marshall, the posse again got into a firefight with the fugitives, but the exchange of fire took place at about three hundred yards and nobody was hurt. The posse lost the trail again after that, but did not give up. The local Anti-Horsethief Association set about warning ranchers and farmers in the area, but the outlaws stole still another team from a farmer and rustled a batch of spareribs the farmer's wife had cooked for her husband. The pursuers found the farmer's buggy broken down and abandoned and tracked the outlaws farther, following discarded sparerib bones.

The robbery had occurred on a Monday night. On Saturday the chase was still on, and still another inconclusive gunfight with lawmen took place near tiny Isabella. Again nobody was hurt and the robbers broke contact, stole more horses the next morning, and ran again, all the way down into the Texas Panhandle.

Exactly where the brothers rode is unknown, but history does show that they rendezvoused with Richard Simmons, who had deserted his family down in Logan County. Instead of putting Oklahoma far behind them, the outlaws moved their base of operations into the rugged Osage. The Osage country was thinly settled, tangled, and a difficult land that had been and would remain an outlaw haven. It was a country of rock and thick groves of trees, brush, and ravines, a very bad place from which to root out armed fugitives.

The gang made quite a splash with their next undertaking. They found a spot along the road between Bartlesville and Pawhuska and robbed one traveler after another, Simmons guarding each one of their victims in a thicket of trees while the Martins watched the road for more travelers. Among the victims was former deputy marshal, Dave Ware, traveling with his wife.

Sam Martin recognized Ware and crowed, "You're a killer; why don't you do something?"

Ware wasn't having any. "To hell with you," he said. "You've got the drop and I have no gun." And he added ominously, "I'll wait."

But the bandits had more plans for evil. One of their victims was driving by in a hay wagon, which the Martins soon turned into a barricade across the road. By six in the evening, the bandits had collected an astonishing bevy of captives, some one hundred men, women, and children. They also had fifty-five or so horses, not to mention buggies, wagons, and the like. It had been quite an afternoon and the outlaws disappeared again, moving far to the west.

Their next target was the tiny town of Hopeton, a hamlet south of Alva, and there they invaded a combination store and post office, stealing about $100, a batch of postage stamps, and some clothing. They took a couple of shots at a man driving by in his wagon when he would not stop. They missed him, and he clattered off down the street. The robbers fled, and this time they had about a ten-hour start on a pursuing posse. Again they disappeared, only to surface near the thriving railroad hub of Geary.

Geary had two banks, and somebody was building another one. It even rose to the dignity of having a good-sized hotel and, of all things, an opera house. It had its tough side, too, plenty of gin mills and plenty of violence. Such a tough town required tough law enforcement, and Geary had exactly that.

The city marshal, John Cross, was quite a character, hardy and courageous, and, well, the epitome of the Western movie lawman. When Cross became a little dry, he would ride his horse into a saloon, collect a beer, and ride on out the back door. Even with his little peccadilloes, he was a popular man.

The Martins and their hanger-on Simmons had their eyes on the town's twin banks, but their appearance aroused some suspicion. A young farmer spotted them on his way into town but did not recognize them for what they were. He did, however, remember that one man carried a beautiful Colt with stag horn grips. Neither the farmer nor another man who saw the gang was entirely satisfied with their appearance, and they intended to tell Marshal Cross about the strangers the next day.

But that night Cross failed to come home to his farm outside of town. When he was about four hours overdue, his worried wife saw his horse come home, without its rider but with a bullet wound. She telephoned the town, and people turned out and began to look for him. They found him dead, shot through the body, and they also found what remained of a fire and signs that three men had been there. The inescapable conclusion was that the marshal, doing his job, had ridden up to the fire and simply been shot down.

A large posse gave chase, led by Sheriff Ozmun of neighboring Canadian County. The trail led off south toward the town of Anadarko. While the posse was on the trail, rewards totaling $1,350 were offered by the territorial government, the county, the local Independent Order of Odd Fellows (IOOF) lodge, and the Anti-Horsethief Association.

For two weeks lawmen pursued the gang, running down reports of sightings. It was learned that the outlaws had intended to stop and rob a Santa Fe train but called off their attempt when they learned that the train carried guards. They contented themselves with robbing a cowboy at the 101 Ranch and pushing on.

And then the officers got a break, a report that the outlaws had returned to the rugged Osage country. There are several versions of how this came about—that the news was passed along by an Indian who had fed the three, by cowboys who recognized them, by a doctor, by women sent by the foreman of a cow camp where the gang had bullied the camp cook into providing them meals.

Once in the Osage the posse discovered the outlaws with help from a group of Osage Indians. These Indians watched a heavily armed white man come down to a creek to draw water. One of the Osages followed him some eight miles, then rode into Pawhuska to find deputy Indian Agency police chief Wiley Haines, who also carried a commission as a deputy US marshal. The Indian reported what he had seen to Haines and drew a little map of the location of the outlaws.

Haines collected Osage chief of police Warren Bennett and Indian policeman Henry Majors. The three officers rode casually out of Pawhuska and headed for a piece of high ground deep in the ravine of Bird Creek. The little knob of ground, thick with brush, was called Wooster Mound. The lawmen timed their arrival to reach the area at dusk and in the failing light dismounted behind the last ridge between them and Wooster Mound.

Crawling forward to the ridgeline, they found the outlaws relaxed, one man watching the horses while the other two hunkered down behind a pile of saddles and other gear and cooked something over a small fire. Much later, a Lawton deputy named Woody added a few details to the story. The officers saw the smoke from the outlaws' fire, he said, and crawled closer to find their quarry dining on grilled meat.

One of the bandits' horses saw or smelled Haines. The beast snorted, and the fight was on. Sam Martin grabbed his rifle and sprang to his feet, already firing, while his brother grabbed his own weapon and made a run for the creek. Haines and Bennett stood up and charged into the open, firing as they came.

Haines hit Will in the leg and then hit him again in the corner of his mouth, a bullet that also removed a substantial portion of the back of his head. He fell into a ditch, quite dead. Meanwhile, Bennett was shooting at Sam, hitting him in the wrist and in the right shoulder, a round that continued on to exit from his chest. Sam went down as well, falling in a patch of shade, unmoving.

Haines pulled his revolver and cautiously approached the motionless outlaw. But then, as Haines got close, Sam Martin rolled over and fired. Haines started to jump away when he saw Martin begin to move, which may have saved the lawman's life. As it was, the wound he received was ugly. The soft-nosed slug tore into his shoulder and swerved toward the back of his neck, leaving a deadly trail of fragments from the bullet's copper jacket. Some of the fragments scattered into the officer's right lung, tearing at the blood vessels.

As Haines fell, Bennett rushed past him, kicking the outlaw's rifle away and promising a bullet between the eyes if Martin tried anything more. Meanwhile, Simmons was running for his life. Officer Major pulled down on the man with his rifle and the bandit fell. But he immediately jumped up and continued running.

In reporting the battle the *Oklahoma Daily Capital* noted that the combatants had fired a total of twenty-seven rounds in a single minute and lauded the "[t]hree brave and nervy officers who took on three desperadoes who had sworn never to be taken alive."

The Osages, still in their nearby camp, appeared and loaded Sam Martin and the badly wounded Haines into a wagon. Bennett performed some crude emergency surgery on his deputy, cutting at least some of the rifle bullet out of his shoulder. Haines was still in desperate straits, however, and needed immediate medical attention.

Bennett and Majors collected the booty, three horses (all stolen), a heap of tack (also stolen), weapons, camping gear, and some thousand rounds of ammunition. Prominent among the captured weapons was Sam's fancy Colt revolver with its stag horn grips. The lawmen also found Sheriff Cross's star and silver watch, both stolen from the fallen lawman.

Haines teetered on the edge of eternity but slowly improved.

Not so for Sam Martin. As he slowly sank, Sam told the law all about the gang's depredations. He told of the Hennessey robbery and the murder of Gus Cravatt, the wild afternoon of multiple robberies on the Bartlesville road—"more than a hundred people," he said—the robbery of the post office and store at Hopeton. He could not resist boasting that he, his brother, and Simmons had robbed "more people than any gang in history."

But then, as he looked death in the face, he added, "I guess I've been on the wrong trail."

There was, as the *State Capital* put it, "great rejoicing" among the populace at the extirpation of the Martin boys, and the remains of the outlaws were hauled into Guthrie so that their identity could be confirmed. A number of their victims identified the corpses as the men who had robbed them.

They were carted off to the ministrations of Patterson Brothers, undertakers, and the *State Capital* again waxed eloquent:

> After years of running amuck . . . committing
> innumerable robberies and staining their hands with
> human blood . . . Sam and Will Martin are lying side by
> side in the dead house, with eyes forever closed . . . ghastly
> wounds where their young lives went out in a hopeless
> struggle to take by force what could much easier have
> been won by honest toil.

If the paper's prose was a trifle florid, the moral it drew was absolutely right. What now remained was disposing of what was left. Their father sent a message that he couldn't manage to take care of the bodies and added "dispose of them by law." Whatever he meant by that, the *State Capital* added, "[T]hey have already been disposed of according to law. . . . [T]hey will now be disposed of according to custom."

That meant potter's field in the Guthrie cemetery where they would share space with, among other felons, Bill Doolin and Little Dick West. In time they would be joined by Elmer McCurdy, who would pull down the tone of the neighborhood.

Meanwhile, tough Wiley Haines continued to improve. The doctors had dug out most of the copper fragments, and he could enjoy himself reading through piles of congratulatory letters and a special commendation from the US attorney. Bennett received two-thirds of the reward offered after the murder of Cross, and he split the sum with Haines and policeman Majors.

All of which left Simmons as the only loose end of the Martin Gang, with a third part of the reward waiting for anyone who could bring him down. The law thought they had him that autumn when a man supposed to be Simmons was arrested in Galena, Kansas. The man turned out not to be Simmons, but the arrest was not all bad. The man was described by the *State Capital* as an "all-around bad man" wanted down in the territory, whither he was promptly sent.

In April of 1919 Simmons was captured in Boonville, Missouri, living under another name. A great deal of time had passed since the gang's heyday, however, and the remaining witnesses could no longer make positive identifications. But the federal authorities had not forgotten Simmons, and Haines was the key, picking him out from a crowd of almost a hundred people.

Now he faced a federal jury, accused of assault with intent to commit murder that day at Wooster Mound. After a hard-fought trial, in which the defense's alibi was supported by witnesses from Florida, Simmons—or Smith, as he now called himself—was released after the jury could not agree. The case remained open, but no further trial was convened.

And in the autumn of 1928, as he was running hard for sheriff of Osage County at the age of sixty-eight, Wiley Haines collapsed on the courthouse steps with a massive heart attack. He was dead in just a few minutes. Now he could not testify against Simmons ever again, and the assault case withered away.

Haines, the dedicated lawman, was honored with a fitting epitaph: AN HONEST MAN IS THE NOBLEST WORK OF GOD. It fit the man.

Nobody knows what happened to Simmons.

When George Birdwell Robbed the Wrong Bank

The Usual Hazards of Daylight Banditry

The gang drove into Boley and turned up Main Street, and Pete Glass stopped the Buick, pointing north, just south of the bank. Glass waited in the car while George Birdwell and Champ Patterson got out, Birdwell carrying a 1911 Colt .45 semiautomatic pistol, Patterson with a sawed-off shotgun beneath his overcoat. As they entered the bank, treasurer Wesley Riley looked up from his conversation with Horace Aldridge, suspecting nothing. D. J. Turner, the president, got up from his desk and moved up behind the bars on the teller's window to serve Birdwell. He found himself looking into the bad end of the Colt pistol.

"We're robbing this bank," Birdwell said. "Hand over the dough! Don't pull no alarm!"

Turner said nothing but began to pull bills out of the cash drawer, sliding them under the bars to the bandit. Meanwhile, bookkeeper Herb McCormick saw what was going on, slid softly to the floor, and crawled back toward the vault, hoping to get to the rifle he kept there. And then, as Turner pulled out the last bills in the drawer, the alarm fired with a deafening din, both inside the bank and outside, and in the four other stores wired into the system. "You pulled that alarm," yelled Birdwell. "I'll kill you for that!"

And the doughty Turner looked the bandit right in the eye: "You bet I pulled it!"

Riley, standing helplessly in front of Patterson's shotgun, saw what was coming. "Don't hurt nobody, please!" he pleaded, but his only answer was obscenities. Infuriated by Turner's defiance, Birdwell's mercurial temper exploded, and he drove four .45 slugs into Turner at point-blank range. Turner staggered back and went down, clutching at the desk for support as he fell.

McCormick reached the vault and his rifle, and, as the bank president fell, the bookkeeper put a bullet into Birdwell's neck. Blood spurting from the wound, the outlaw dropped his pistol and the sack full of about $700 in loot. "I'm shot," he cried, no longer bold and arrogant. "Hold me! I'm . . . " And down he went.

Patterson ordered Riley and customer Aldridge to pull what was left of Birdwell to the bank door and get him outside. Under the malignant stare of the shotgun, they did. Glass, hearing the firing, now came running into the bank, pistol in hand. He fired random shots toward the back of the bank as he and Patterson fell back toward the door, still trying to scoop up bills scattered across the counter and floor and stuff them into their pockets.

Outside, the outlaws saw citizens headed their way, running toward the bank, carrying rifles and shotguns. The hostages took advantage of the confusion of their captors to drop what was left of Birdwell on the sidewalk and run for it, disappearing down a side street. Riley's coat was ripped by a bullet or buckshot aimed at Patterson, but both he and Aldridge escaped without being hurt.

His forced labor and human shields suddenly gone, Patterson bent over to pick up Birdwell. Hazel, who owned the town's big department store, had told the sheriff he and his shotgun were ready for a bank robbery, that he might "git me a pretty boy for breakfast." Now he took a shot at Patterson.

Glass crawled toward Birdwell, as Patterson saw shopkeeper Hazel on his store's veranda and fired at him. Glass realized that Birdwell was quite dead and saw the giant form of Sheriff McCormick heading for him, followed by more citizens who had armed themselves at the Masonic Temple. Glass, seeing that the fat was in the fire, abandoned Birdwell's corpse and ran to the Buick. Patterson, stubborn or stupid, or both, was still tugging at Birdwell's corpse when a citizen named Zeigler shot him again.

Miraculously untouched by the hailstorm of lead, Glass slammed the Buick into reverse and began to turn around and make tracks for the highway. At this point, enter retired sheriff John Owens. Kneeling in the center of Main Street some fifty yards from the Buick, Owens coolly put a bullet into Glass. Roaring backward, the car crashed into a parking lot wall and stopped. Everybody within range poured bullets into it until the car was junk and Glass was a corpse. Birdwell and his boys had taken on the wrong town.

In 1932 Boley's five-block Main Street boasted forty stores, including Hazel's two-story department store and the Farmers' and Merchants' Bank. Boley was a successful all-black community, one of about two dozen such towns in Oklahoma in those days. Across the street from the bank stood the Masonic Temple, an impressive three-story structure. The bank, whose president, Turner, had also served as mayor for ten years, was the town's centerpiece. He had been worried about bank robbery, with good reason.

In the first three months of 1932, bandits stuck up Oklahoma banks for some $62,000, a lot of money to small depositors. In Boley a hoodlum named Charles Arthur Floyd began to create a reputation for himself. He was called "Choc" by his friends, but the rest of the reading public called him "Pretty Boy."

Then and later, people who should have known better called Floyd a latter-day Robin Hood. They gave no thought to the little people whose savings were wiped out by his raids. There was no friendly FDIC to protect depositors if a bank was driven to bankruptcy by robbers, because unless the bank had insurance, the depositors were out of luck.

Floyd and his gang had already struck the banks at Paden and Prague, not far away from Boley, and they robbed both in the same day. And just the last January, a gang had robbed the bank in the little town of Castle, just six miles down the road from Boley.

Turner said flatly that he would defend the town's savings at all costs. When Turner said something, he meant it. His bank had installed a brand-new electric alarm system. It triggered automatically when the last bills were removed from a teller's drawer, whether the bills were snatched by a robber or removed under duress by a bank employee.

The alarm made a noise like the last trumpet and was tied into four businesses in downtown Boley: Hazel's department store, Shorty Bragg's barbershop, Aldridge's pool hall, and John Owens's meat market.

Butcher John Owens was a formidable man indeed, a retired peace officer who always wore a black Stetson with a bullet hole in the crown, a memento of a gunfight. He and other citizens of Boley kept their shotguns and rifles close at hand, and more weapons were stashed in the Masonic Temple.

Anybody who tried to hold up the bank would also have to come through Sheriff Lankston McCormick, all six foot seven of him, very tough and very capable. Anyone who wanted the hard-earned money of Boley's people would have to buck most of the rest of Boley's determined citizenry as well. But George Birdwell didn't have the sense to stay away.

Companion and sometime accomplice to Pretty Boy Floyd, Birdwell was later described by a lawman as "the man who planned these activities and handled the machine gun in their raids." Birdwell had been a cowboy and an oil field roustabout. At least one story relates that at one time he was even a church deacon. Whatever Birdwell's history, he had turned robber, presumably because there was more money in the larceny business. Birdwell was a veteran criminal and well known for his volatile temper. He nevertheless had the reputation of being a devoted father, who not only took care of his wife and his own four children but also looked after his two nephews.

Nobody knows for sure how many banks Birdwell and Pretty Boy Floyd stuck up together. They robbed the bank of little Morris a couple of times, and banks in Shamrock, Konawa, Maud, Earlsboro, and Tahlequah, in addition to the banks in Paden and Castle. They held up the American State Bank in Henryetta, Oklahoma, early in November 1932 and got more than $11,000, a notable haul for those impoverished days.

Of Birdwell's helpers at Boley, Champ Patterson was an experienced outlaw, and Birdwell's brand-new bank robber was a black gambler from Boley called Pete Glass. It may have been Glass who suggested the Boley raid to Birdwell, for the cocky Glass boasted that he was going to "show the gang how to rob a colored bank."

Pretty Boy Floyd refused to join in the Boley venture. This disappointed Birdwell, but it certainly didn't stop him. He decided to take on the Farmers' and Merchants' Bank by himself, with only the two men he had.

Two days before Thanksgiving, Birdwell and his cohorts drove their big black Buick down to Boley to reconnoiter the town and its bank. They hung out at Horace Aldridge's pool hall, shooting a few games and watching the bank across the street. Neither Birdwell nor the rest of the bandits aroused suspicion until they left town. They made the mistake of saying something ungentlemanly to Bennie Dolphin, a pretty secretary who worked for Dr. W. A. Paxton, whose office was across the street from the bank.

After breakfast the next day, allowing time for the Boley bank to open, the three climbed in their Buick. Patterson, who usually drove the getaway car, took the wheel, but somewhere near Boley, he moved over so that Glass could drive. The outlaws' plan—insofar as they had any plan at all—was to drive up Main Street and stop just short of the bank. They would park on the wrong side of the street, pointed north, the direction away from the highway.

Once Patterson and Birdwell had the cash and returned to the Buick, Glass was to back up a short distance, making a U-turn as he did so, and then drive hard to the south, to the highway and safety. It would have made more sense to park facing south to begin with and save a few precious seconds when they ran. The right side of the car would face the bank, giving the men two doors to jump into instead of just one.

It was the day before Thanksgiving, and many farmers were in town to buy supplies. Some bought shotgun ammunition because quail season opened the following day. Also in the bank was Herb McCormick, the bookkeeper and brother of Sheriff Lank McCormick, and the bank's treasurer Wesley W. Riley, who was talking to Horace Aldridge, a customer. Out on the street, Sheriff McCormick was making his rounds, dressed in high boots with his trousers stuffed into them, a plaid shirt under a sheepskin coat, and a cowboy hat on top.

Now the robbery had been defeated in blood, and the sheriff shouted for a cease-fire. Dr. Paxton ran across Main Street toward the bank, his shotgun in one hand and his medical bag in the other. Turner was semiconscious on the floor, soaked in blood. Herb McCormick knelt beside him, unable to help.

Turner, still clinging to life, was loaded into Dr. Paxton's car for the trip to the hospital at Okemah. Turner's wife drove up and jumped into Paxton's vehicle, but neither her love nor the doctor's ministrations could save the gallant bank president. He died on the road.

Patterson survived his multiple wounds to reach Okemah.

The next day, according to the *Daily Oklahoman*, Champ Patterson, unable to talk because of his neck wound, confirmed by nodding his head that the dead bandit was the infamous George Birdwell.

A crowd of over five thousand people turned out for Turner's funeral on November 28. Boley was jammed with mourners, only about a quarter of whom could crowd inside the church for the funeral services. Among those offering eulogies was a man representing the Oklahoma Bankers Association. Scattered through the crowd were more than fifty peace officers in plain clothes, alert to the possibility that Floyd might "come to claim revenge," as one paper put it.

Pretty Boy Floyd didn't show up. He left the state before the year was out, never to return except to get himself buried at the biggest funeral ever seen in Oklahoma. Within two years he would be cut down by lawmen in the dirt of an Ohio cornfield.

In addition to laudatory letters, Herb McCormick also received a $500 reward from the Oklahoma Bankers Association for killing Birdwell, and Boley's "vigilance committee" got another $500 for exterminating Glass. Governor "Alfalfa Bill" Murray invited Herb McCormick to Oklahoma City, where the governor conferred on him the honorary title of "Major."

So he was known for the rest of his life.

The Saga of Zip Wyatt
Worthless

Zip Wyatt, aka "Wild Charlie" or "Dick Yeager," was an outlaw almost from birth, but never more than a small-time hoodlum under any of his various names. He specialized in country stores and such—easy targets where you were unlikely to meet inconvenient people like men wearing stars. He hit rural post offices, too, which were often part of a store. Such places often had registered mail around, and that meant money.

He'd never get rich on such robberies, because the targets were mostly vulnerable mom-and-pop operations. Zip's chief claim to fame was his absolutely amoral view of the world, which meant he was not bothered by almost any sort of dishonesty . . . including killing people.

He got together a gang, a few punks like himself, and they became known around Oklahoma's Gyp Hills as the Wyatt-Black Gang. Gang members came and went, but at the heart of the gang were just four second-rate criminals.

The Black in the gang's name was one Isaac Black, called Ike, and the rest of the dubious personnel were Black's wife, Belle, and Zip's comfort woman, Jenny Freeman, wayward wife to an ex-member of the gang.

Zip came of second-rate stock, a reliable prediction of a criminal career. His father, known as "Old Six" or "Six-shooter Bill," was much dedicated to sampling strong spirits in large quantities—a habit that got him lodged with some frequency in

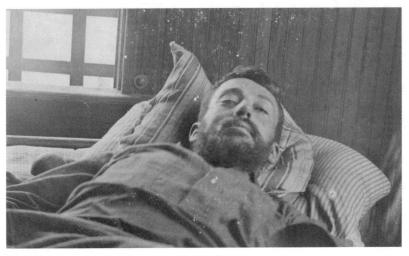

Dick Yeager, alias Zip Wyatt, in Enid jail
Western History Collections, University of Oklahoma Libraries

the Guthrie jail. An older brother, "Six-shooter Jack," made his living gambling until he came in second in an 1891 bar-room fight in Texline, Texas.

"Six-shooter Bill," along with his wife, Rachel Jane, and their eight offspring moved from Indiana to Oklahoma in 1889, and settled in a spot on Antelope Creek called Cowboy Flat. Cowboy Flat is an area of some 10,000 acres of fine land in a big bend of the Cimarron River near the towns of Guthrie and Langston. Drained by two creeks, it was a good country for both crops and cattle, so it naturally became a stop on the long road north to the railhead towns of Kansas.

In 1880 and after, the Halsell brothers—famous stockmen— began to drive huge herds into the area, still technically owned by the Creek Nation. Among their cowboys were a number of embryo outlaws, names to be famous before too long, men like Bill Doolin, Little Dick West, Dick Broadwell, Bill Powers, and Bitter Creek Newcomb, all of whom died young of bullet disease. When the area was finally opened for settlement, some of these hard cases established claims there. Most of the rest of the other settlers, however, were simply honest folk looking for a new life in a place they could call their own.

Enter Zip Wyatt. It is scant wonder that Zip grew up wild, given to shooting up things that weren't his while full to overflowing with ol' devil John Barleycorn. There is a story that he acquired his nickname Zip from his agility in staying one jump ahead of the law.

So far, his actions had been little more than the antics of a wild kid. But then, in November of 1889, two masked men tried to hold up the Santa Fe office north of Guthrie. When the telegraph operator laughed at what he thought was a joke, one of the punks drove a Winchester slug through him. The bandits fled empty-handed, leaving the operator with only life enough to telegraph for help. He was found dead with his hand still on the key.

Zip was the killer, although that was not discovered until much later in his wild career. Then, in June of 1891, Zip and his brother-in-law Charley Bailey celebrated something-or-other by shooting up the little town of Mulhall. The citizens took umbrage, and a gunfight followed as Zip took horse and fled; two citizens were wounded in the exchange.

Once again, Zip ran for it, surfacing in Greenburg, Kansas, where he stole a watch and other articles from a livery stable owner, and then went on to Pryor's Grove, where a number of residents were celebrating the Glorious Fourth. It was quite a do, featuring a hot-air balloon; various side-show performers; and The Great Gamboni, who rode a bicycle on a tightrope to thrill the yokels.

Deputy Sheriff Andy Balfour went to Pryor's Grove to serve a warrant on Zip. But when he called to Zip that he had a warrant for his arrest, Zip snapped, "And I have this for you." Wheeling around, Zip shot Balfour through the body, breaking his spine; dying, Balfour shot Zip twice, inflicting only superficial wounds.

Zip jumped on his horse and ran for it, spraying bullets back at the crowd. The Great Gamboni, yelling and pointing at the retreating outlaw, fell off his wire, bike and all, when the milling crowd ran into his guy lines.

So Zip was on the run again, this time with a reward on his head; he headed for what once had been home country, Indiana, but was captured by Terre Haute officers at his aunt's home. And he started to go for his pistol, but thought better of it when he felt the barrels of a lawman's shotgun in his belly.

And now a wrangle developed between Kansas, which wanted him for murder, and Oklahoma officers, who had a warrant for him for the Mulhall attack. While the legal niceties were being thrashed out, Zip crawled through a sewer pipe in a part of the Guthrie jail still under construction—legend had it that he made his break during a Salvation Army service—and was picked up with a team and wagon driven by his sister. In any case, he was long gone.

The result of this crime and escape was the Wyatt-Black Gang, and a word is in order about the "molls" of the group. Belle Black was neither attractive nor slim, while Jenny Freeman was tall and skinny. Jenny had been the wife of Matt Freeman, who had sheltered Zip after his escape from the Guthrie jail. By way of gratitude, Zip made off with his wife.

The women's service, besides the obvious, was to case potential targets, finding out whether there were weapons behind the counter and so on, and to help with the getaway afterward. If they only helped as scouts and getaway helpers, that was certainly valuable.

But most of all they were female, which counted for quite a lot as a comfort to the outlaws holed up in the Gypsum Hills, a wild, cedar-covered tangle of high ground across old Woods County. The Gyp Hills, also called the Glass Mountains because their mineral deposits sometimes shimmered in sunlight, were the perfect hideout.

By this time Zip was calling himself Dick Yeager, and was acquiring a sort of gang. Besides the women and Black, a weak reed at best, there was Mexican John, a sometime barber, and Jim Umbra, an undistinguished badman whose trade was rustling. Umbra and Mexican John eventually turned to stealing other people's cows in 1895, but were run down and summarily hanged by pursuing cowboys.

Another suspected gang member named Wentworth shot Deputy Marshal Forrest Halsell in the gun hand, knocking his six-gun away, but Halsell was made of stern stuff: Operating left-handed, he opened Wentworth up with a heavy sheath knife. Wentworth survived the grisly wound, but went off to prison.

Zip's raids became enough of an annoyance to the stock men and storekeepers of the region that chapters of the Anti-Horsethief Association began to pop up. One raid, an attempt to rustle Cheyenne horses, was driven back in confusion into the Gyp Hills by none other than Chief Roman Nose and a band of his braves.

Just which crimes the gang committed gets a little confusing. Once outlaws began to get a reputation, crimes were attributed to them that in fact belonged to somebody else less famous. One they certainly committed was a robbery in Arapaho in November of 1893. They did well on that one, pilfering more than $700 and a watch, plus blankets and canned goods. The next robbery took place at a village called Todd, and began when one bandit asked for supper. In those days people fed a hungry stranger, and the gang paid for their hospitality by killing the store owner, Ed Townsend.

Townsend put up a fight, knocking one outlaw down with an iron bar; even though Townsend was shot though both wrists and disabled, the outlaws shot him twice more. It was a pointless, spiteful, cold-blooded murder. The county residents spoke meaningfully of lynching, could they ever come up with the outlaws.

Then there were the jobs they might have pulled, but probably didn't. Among these was a train robbery at a place called Pond Creek in the spring of 1894. Somebody surely stuck up the Rock Island, and at least six men participated, firing a stick of dynamite under the car and gaining entry. But the canny express guard, Jake Harmon, walked through the train, having left the express car through the back door. Harmon emerged into the darkness, saw a bandit pointing a pistol toward the express car, and shot him down. The robber expired on the spot, and the others fled. A posse arrived shortly thereafter and captured another of the bandits.

Maybe Zip and Isaac Black were involved in this one, but probably not. Zip was at least experienced enough to know that there would be a rear door to the express car and to choose a more appropriate spot for the holdup; the Pond Creek fiasco was attempted on flat prairie, without cover of any kind. It does not sound like a Zip Wyatt operation.

Zip and his cohorts developed another crooked hospitality scam. Stopping at a farmhouse, they would ask for a meal, and afterward offer a large bill in payment, knowing full well the farmer would not be able to change that kind of money. Well, said Zip, how much *do* you have? And when the answer came, no matter what it was, robbery followed. On one occasion the gang robbed an old soldier of his entire month's pension. Zip and Black bore not the slightest resemblance to Robin Hood.

At last the law had some luck, when two deputy sheriffs and a pair of deputy marshals ran down the gang in the Gyp Hills. A long gunfight followed, in which Zip was shot in the arm and Black in the heel before both men escaped. The officers captured all their camp equipment, some horse furniture, and, most important, Belle and Jenny as they ran from a dugout the foursome had occupied.

The lawmen dragged the girls off to jail. Defiant and singularly unpleasant to the end, they were carrying loot from a post-office robbery and photos of the deputies who had killed Tulsa Jack Blake. They had defaced the pictures, maybe in an attempt at voodoo revenge. Zip and Black remained free, but an estimated two hundred men were searching the countryside for them, giving them no respite.

Even under the ceaseless pressure of the law's pursuit, the outlaws proclaimed their intent to break their honeys from durance vile. That stupid scheme fell apart when jilted husband Matt Freeman learned of their intention and warned the authorities. The plan, such as it was, called for Zip to ride into town at night with Black as a "prisoner" in handcuffs, capture the jailer, cut the telephone line, and gallop off with the women.

It was about as realistic as the tale of the Tooth Fairy to begin with. And, on observing the jail was heavily guarded, the outlaws decided common sense was miles ahead of chivalry and derring-do, and snuck away into the night. It's a good story, anyway.

The chase continued. Acting on several tips, officers followed a two-gun rider to his meeting with a wagon, stepped out, and summoned the man to surrender. Why gosh, fellers, the man said, I'm just a peaceful citizen, or words to that effect, all the while edging toward the wagon, from which two men then jumped and opened fire on the officers, one trying to hold the frantic team and shoot at the same time. It was a bad idea.

The man who tried to hold the horses was shot through the arm, dropped his pistol, and ran a little way before the officers ran him down. The horse rider took a bullet that pierced the horse's neck and hit the man in the chest; both of them died in the dust of the road. The third man, hit in the thigh, called it quits.

The three were innocent citizens, the survivors said, who opened fire at what they thought were bandits. And indeed they were not the posse's intended quarry, although some question was raised because they fired first; because one of the surviving citizens refused to identify himself; and because the three were carrying five rifles, three pistols, and about five hundred rounds of ammunition.

At any rate, the posse's quarry stayed on the loose. Their next foray was into the little town of Oxley, where they robbed a storekeeper-postmaster of a few dollars, some tobacco, and canned goods. Despite their searching and threats, the money bag remained obscured under the horse trough, where the merchant had thoughtfully pushed it.

Disappointed, the robbers went over the list of callers at the post office, and actually invaded the homes of a couple of them, suspecting money was in the registered letters they had signed for. But again, if the registered letters had contained money, the bandits couldn't find it, and the two turned north toward the Gyp Hills and safety. They hadn't counted on the posse that came upon them on the way. A ferocious battle followed, but the outlaws slipped away; Black with a minor head wound, all their gear left behind.

Another posse followed, and found Zip and Black "holed up in a canyon." One posse man was shot through the thigh, and the two outlaws broke free, riding two of the posse's stampeded horses. Another man was sure he had hit Zip, but thought the outlaw must have been wearing "a shield over his body."

For the moment their prey had eluded them, but the officers did not rest. Somebody had seen the outlaws desperately fleeing, Zip trailing and whipping Black's horse. Obviously, their mounts were about worn out. Finally the two stopped at an isolated house and asked for food. The lady of the house fed them, but when they asked about fresh horses, they were told there were none to be had.

Meanwhile, a posse under Deputy Sheriff Marion Hildreth closed in; they had spotted the fugitives' exhausted horses tied at the house well, and as they watched, Black and Zip came out of the house, arguing over possession of the remains of their chewing tobacco. The officers' commands to surrender were met with gunfire, and Hildreth put a rifle bullet through Black's head. Exit Ike.

Zip was hit in the chest, a slug that hit close to the nipple and plowed a furrow around his body. He ran then, bolting into a nearby cornfield, shouting "Hildreth, you have killed the best man in Oklahoma!" obviously a considerable exaggeration when applied to Black. The posse shot at him, but did not follow, probably out of concern for their wounded member and to secure Ike Black's remains, which was required for the reward.

Zip's next stop was at the home of doctor, whom he forced to repair his wound . . . and then, as usual the soul of gratitude, he stole the doctor's horse. The pursuit continued as Zip wore out one horse after another. At last two officers found the badly hurt, very tired man lying on his back in a cornfield, a Winchester on one side of him, a Colt on the other. In spite of his bloody record, the two deputies called to Zip to surrender.

Zip's response was to grab for his revolver, and both officers fired at once. Both slugs hit Zip in the belly, in the area of the hip, only a couple of inches apart. At last Zip surrendered. "For God's sake, don't kill me," he pleaded, no longer the cocky outlaw.

The lawmen took what care they could of the outlaw, until a wagon was found to carry him to shelter at the church in Sheridan. It was Sunday, and services had just ended. The church bulletin board laid across a couple of pews served as a rough bed, and medical help was called. Two local doctors responded—one or both might have been part of the congregation—and opined that while the outlaw was badly wounded, the damage might not be fatal.

There followed an unseemly wrangle between posses over possession of Zip. The question was, who was to have the reward for him, to the point at which Zip commented, "If you'll give me my six-shooter for about two seconds I'll stop the argument." A wire to a federal judge produced an order that Zip be delivered to federal authorities, but that was ignored by the county posse men, who agreed at last to split the reward.

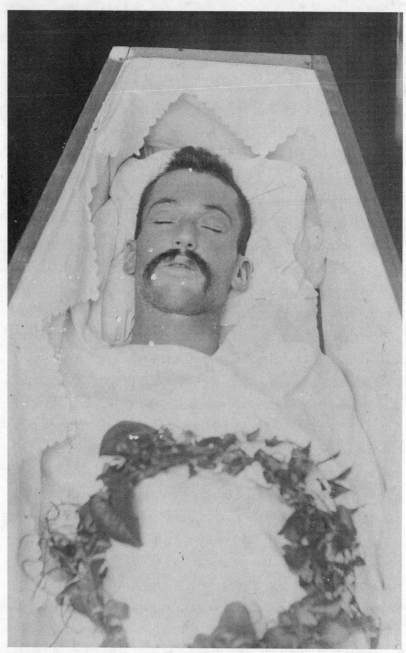

Zip Wyatt in his casket
Western History Collections, University of Oklahoma Libraries

And so Zip ended up in the Garfield County jail in Enid, where there was more medical examination. The Enid doctors waxed far more pessimistic than the first examiners, giving Zip only a 10 percent chance of survival. The two bullets in his belly had hit around the pelvis and ranged upward, and the doctors could not even find them. All that could be done for Zip was to keep him full of morphine and hope for the best.

And for a while it looked like he might miraculously pull through. Deputy Marshal Chris Madsen paid a call on him and afterward telegraphed his deputy in Guthrie: "It's Zip all right. He asks to have his father notified and come here quick as he cannot live."

Even so, when the marshal approached his bed, Zip tried to snatch Madsen's pistol and commented after Madsen jumped back, "I guess that'll be my last chance." He was right. Zip did pay the lawman a sort of left-handed compliment as Madsen left: "If there had not been worse men on my track than Madsen," he said somewhat obscurely, "I would never have been captured."

He did manage to rally enough to partake of fried chicken and other delicacies, and put on a regular show for hundreds of visitors, including bragging that he had killed eleven men; that was something of an embroidery on his real score, to be sure, but it thrilled the callers.

For a time, Zip appeared to have a chance to cheat death. As one paper reported, "He seems to grow stronger on his diet of musket balls and resolutely defies the grim specter, much to the surprise of the medical men who pronounced his case hopeless." But the apparent rally was illusory, a sort of calm before the storm.

While he lasted, Zip was great copy for the papers, right down to edifying reports about the nonfunctioning of his urinary tract and bowels, and the fact that he drank much milk plus four bottles of beer a day. But gradually he began to sink.

Blood poisoning set in, normally the kiss of death in those pre-antibiotic days, and the doctors could see the end coming. As they later learned during the autopsy, Zip's pelvic bone had almost disintegrated—it was in at least fifty pieces—and the lining of his stomach had turned black. At that, Zip had lasted a phenomenal thirty-five days before the Grim Reaper got him.

He was buried in a cheap wooden coffin in a potter's field. It wasn't much of a send-off: There were no mourners, and even Zip's father, "Six-shooter Bill," failed to show, which shouldn't have surprised anybody.

As to the women, according to one source, a grand jury refused to indict them. Another says they got short prison terms. In any case, Jenny Freeman apparently at least got religion and traveled about the country preaching the gospel.

As to Belle, stories vary regarding her fate. There is a tale that she remained so depressed over Zip's death that she committed suicide. Another version of her subsequent history has her moving to western Oklahoma, settling down and raising a family. Deputy Marshal Bill Tilghman said that was the case, but as late as 1921 another tale has her moving to Missouri and remarrying.

The usual tales of hidden loot appear in the history of Zip Wyatt and Ike Black, much as they do with almost every other gang. If there is a treasure stashed in a cave in the Gyp Hills, it can't amount to much simply because, for all the misery they caused, and the men they killed, they remained small-time hoodlums.

Not much of an epitaph.

Larry DeVol
Evil Personified

If Zip Wyatt was a simple sociopath, Lawrence DeVol was something infinitely worse. Probably psychotic, DeVol, at the least, would fascinate any psychiatrist and surely was a human organism without any human feeling at all. He only lasted a little more than thirty-one destructive years before he departed this earth, but in that time this hollow man left a trail of death unrivaled in the history of American crime. No doubt organized mobs killed more people over the years, but DeVol was a one-man killing machine.

In addition to robberies, burglaries, and safe-crackings almost innumerable, he is known to have been responsible for the deaths of eleven people, six of whom were lawman. There likely were more corpses littered along his back trail, because he was suspected in other killings, including contract assassinations.

He was Ohio-born back in 1903, and moved with his family to Oklahoma while he was still a child. He apparently grew up fast, so fast that at the tender age of eleven he was consigned as "incorrigible" to something called the Oklahoma State Training School for White Boys.

He spent only a short time at the school, which probably was little more for him than a graduate school in petty crime. In any case, he emerged to become a member of the collection of punks called the Central Park Gang, in Tulsa. Among the other

Larry DeVol, arrested as Leonard Barton,
one of many aliases
Minnesota Historical Society

hoodlum gang members were no less than three of the noxious
Barker brothers, Freddie, Lloyd, and Arthur.

Arrested again at thirteen for larceny, he weathered that rap
and went on studying crime with the gang until he joined three
journeymen holdup men in robbing a bank in Vinton, Iowa.
One of his colleagues was Harvey Bailey, certainly the shrewd-
est, best planner in the robber ranks.

DeVol was learning from the best, but he studiously ignored
one of Bailey's governing rules. Bailey avoided violence whenever possible; he was ready to shoot if he had to, but he was not
a killer. Most of the robbers of the day would use a gun, or a
knife, or a cosh only if they felt compelled to. Larry DeVol was
different; like some of his colleagues in crime, he killed.

But he liked it.

That first robbery produced $70,000, a very great deal of money in the summer of 1927, but it only whetted DeVol's appetite. And so, in the following February, he happily joined in a quarter-million-dollar bank robbery in an Ohio town called Washington Court House.

His career was interrupted temporarily by a conviction for a 1928 robbery gone wrong. He ended up in the Kansas prison at Hutchinson, and there he met his future friend and mentor, Alvin Karpis, sometimes called—for good reason—Creepy Karpis. The pair couldn't wait to resume their life of crime, and so they escaped from prison in March of 1929. Their flight took them through Pueblo, Colorado, where they stole a car and headed for Woodward, Oklahoma.

The pair tried to break into a store in Woodward but managed to bungle that simple operation—vicious the two surely were, but also not very bright. Karpis was arrested and sent back to prison, but DeVol got away.

In the spring of 1930, DeVol was one of two suspects in the callous murder of two out-of-town businessmen in Muskogee. The two elderly easterners were in Oklahoma trying to recover money on mortgages their firm held in the state. The suspicion was that mortgage-holders had hired their assassination.

DeVol was identified as one of the shooters, but once more he escaped retribution, breaking out of jail with another suspect.

That same year he hit a bank with Bailey and four other pros, including journeyman outlaws Frank "Jelly" Nash and Francis Keating. That robbery, in Ottumwa, Iowa, fattened their wallets by some $40,000. The gang hit an even bigger jackpot in September of 1930 with a raid on a bank in Lincoln, Nebraska. That was a fine payday, something in the neighborhood of two and a half million dollars, although most of that was in bonds, not always easy to convert to cash.

DeVol's piece of the loot apparently didn't last long—or maybe he was simply addicted to hurting people—because in November he staged a lone-hand raid on (of all things) a theater in Hannibal, Missouri. Along the way, however, officer George Scrivens and his partner approached DeVol's car and asked him to step out of it.

The response was a hail of .45 slugs, one of which struck Scrivens and knocked him down. DeVol then turned on Scrivens's partner, night marshal John Rose, who was hit twice and went down on the street dying. Scrivens got to his feet, but was hit again high up on one leg. He emptied his pistol at the robber, sadly without hitting anything.

DeVol was long gone, but his fingerprints stayed behind, and from then on he was high on every lawman's list.

He next appeared as a sort of hired gun, a rum-runner on the side, and a killer-for-hire, paid by the piece. Mostly, he worked as an enforcer and is known to have also participated in the beating of a speakeasy owner and the attempted murder of an uncooperative sheriff.

He killed a bootlegger who defied the local booze monopoly, and a second man who also ran an illicit moonshine still. By then the police were turning over every rock searching for him, so DeVol wisely decided another climate would be better for him.

And so he next appeared in St. Paul, Minnesota, where he joined the Barker gang, led by the poisonous Freddie (aka "Shorty") Barker. It was a sort of for-old-times'-sake reunion, for Alvin Karpis was part of the bunch as well, and DeVol had run with Freddie Barker in the gang days in Tulsa. Other big outlaw names worked with the gang from time to time, including Bailey, Keating, and Jelly Nash, one of the dead in the so-called Kansas City Massacre.

And for a time it seemed that this band of punks had found the golden road to riches. They got a quarter of a million dollars from a Minneapolis bank in March of 1932, and $47,000 more a couple of months later in Fort Scott, Kansas. They struck another $250,000 bonanza in Concordia, Kansas, in July, although part of the loot was in bonds.

The next job, in a small town in North Dakota, was a comparative flop, netting only $6,900. DeVol's comrades on that job included Karpis; Freddie Barker; and another dull tool of a Barker kid, christened Arthur, but known in the trade as Doc or Dock (he also, somewhat unoriginally, sometimes called himself Bob Barker, as a sort of unconvincing alias).

This raid was notable for a ferocious reaction by citizens and lawmen, who drove the outlaws out of town in a hail of gunfire. Two women hostages were wounded in the chase, which ended, as usual, at the state line. The gang stole a Minnesota man's automobile and disappeared. The women were left lying in the grass behind a farm building; the police found and rescued them, but it was pure happenstance that they were found at all.

The police found that the car the thugs left behind was especially modified for outlaw work, with an armor to deflect bullets from pursuers and a specially modified back seat that faced to the rear, presumably to accommodate gang members firing on the pursuit.

Before the year was out, DeVol was part of a Minneapolis holdup that produced $22,000 in real money and almost

$100,000 in bonds. Aside from the substantial amount of loot, this job went very wrong indeed: Outside the bank, DeVol killed police officers Leo Gorski and Ira Evans. The two officers had been called by a citizen who correctly suspected that a robbery might be in progress.

The two officers, working together, drove up to the bank, but before they could even get out of their patrol car, DeVol cut loose with a submachine gun at a range of only about fifteen feet. Other gang members fired on the officers from inside the bank, in the process smashing out the bank windows in a shower of glass fragments.

Neither officer had a chance. Evans started to get out the driver's door and draw his pistol, but he never made it, slumping half-in, half-out of the car with his head on the running board. He had been hit ten times. Gorski managed to get out of the car with a shotgun, but he wasn't able to fire a shot. Hit in the chest, stomach, and leg, he collapsed on the pavement.

He was alive, and civilian good Samaritans put him in their car and rushed to the hospital. He arrived still alive and even conscious, but he'd been torn up too badly by outlaw bullets to survive.

That was bad enough, but while the gang was following their standard procedure, moving weaponry and loot to their "switch" getaway car, Freddie Barker killed an unsuspecting citizen. Oscar Erickson, who saw the switch in progress, had slowed down, thinking the men around the two cars might need help.

He got no thanks, just a bullet in the head. He made it to the hospital, but the doctors could not save him either. Because DeVol was part of the same gang, that made him a principal to this murder as well.

The law caught up with Larry DeVol after this one. He was arrested in St. Paul because of his vile temper, when he was found drunk and waving a gun in an apartment building. Two officers arrested him, but only after a violent struggle for the gun. DeVol bit one of the officers during the struggle and was subdued only when a resourceful cop had had enough of wrestling and bashed DeVol in the head with his revolver. Only after the officers won the battle did they find out who they had arrested.

So DeVol celebrated Christmas of 1932 with second-degree murder convictions and a life sentence for the killings of officers Evans and Gorski. He had pleaded guilty to murder, not out of remorse—an emotion entirely alien to him—but to avoid being shipped to Missouri to answer charges for killing another policeman in Kirksville. It was a simple decision: Minnesota had no death penalty; Missouri did.

Off he went to the state prison at Stillwater, Minnesota, longtime home to the Younger brothers after their 1876 disastrous try at robbing the little bank at Northfield. They too went up for murder. Unlike the Youngers, who saw good behavior as a road to freedom, DeVol immediately became a prodigious pain in the behind. He mouthed off regularly at the guard staff and threatened a staff member that he had friends who would "take care of him" and, because he had murdered "one or two," a few more wouldn't matter.

DeVol spent much of 1934 in and out of solitary confinement. He missed the big show on the outside, although he must have heard about it: That was the year the law ran down Pretty Boy Floyd; Bonnie and Clyde; John Dillinger; Baby Face Nelson; and Wilber Underhill, not as well known as the famous "big name" outlaws, but as vile a specimen as DeVol.

None of those stars of the world of crime survived their meetings with the law, which was hardly surprising, given those outlaws' penchant for killing people. In every case the famous names of crime ended up quite dead. No officer wanted to take long chances with his life or his buddies' by prolonged attempts to induce surrender. In some cases, such as the ambush of Bonnie and Clyde, the officers simply blazed away.

DeVol's Tulsa buddies, the venomous Barkers, were winding up their dubious careers about the same time. The matriarch of the clan, Ma Barker (christened, of all things, Arizona Barker), was often cited as the evil criminal genius of the family, but old pro Harvey Bailey, who should know, said otherwise: "That old woman couldn't plan breakfast."

Ma and Arthur went out in a gun battle with the FBI; Herman Barker, another of Ma's poisonous sons, killed himself after he killed an officer and was surrounded by police.

But DeVol wasn't finished. He didn't stay in Stillwater Prison as he was supposed to. Besides threatening the guard staff with murder, he declared he was innocent, and the warden was out to kill him. He said his food was poisoned, among a litany of other complaints.

Either because he put on a convincing act, or because he really wasn't running on all eight cylinders, he was transferred to St. Peter's Hospital for the Criminally Insane. He could not have wished for more. Inevitably, DeVol broke out in 1936, along with some fifteen other more-or-less loony inmates. He promptly returned to what he did best.

Retribution had been a long time coming to Larry DeVol, but it caught up with him after he and another punk robbed a bank in Turon, Kansas. He made a run for Oklahoma, and there the end of the road came in the city of Enid. The police surrounded him in a dive called the German Village Tavern; right in character, DeVol chose to start shooting. Tragically, Officer Cal Palmer died and another lawman was wounded before the remaining officers filled DeVol full of holes . . . lots of them. To everybody's relief, he would remain permanently dead.

There was no noticeable mourning for DeVol's passing. His epitaph, had there been one, would have been simple: GOOD RIDDANCE.

Bibliography

General Reading

Patterson, Richard. *Historical Atlas of the Outlaw West*. Boulder, Colo.: Johnson Books, 1993.

Shirley, Glenn. *Law West of Fort Smith: A History of Frontier Justice in the Indian Territory*. New York: Collier Books, 1957.

————. *West of Hell's Fringe: Crime, Criminals, and the Federal Peace Officer*. Norman: University of Oklahoma Press, 1978.

Smith, Robert Barr. "No God West of Fort Smith." *Wild West* (October 1991).

Bloodbath at Goingsnake

Smith, Robert Barr. "Bloodbath at Going Snake: The Cherokee Courtroom Shootout." *Wild West* (June 2004).

Steele, Phillip. *The Last Cherokee Warriors*. Gretna, La.: Pelican Publishing Company, 1974.

The Cook Gang

Harmon, S. W. *Hell on the Border: He Hanged Eighty-Eight Men*. Muskogee, Okla.: Indian Heritage Association, 1971.

McRae, Bennie J., Jr. *Crawford "Cherokee Bill" Goldsby . . . The Toughest of Them All*. Trotwood, Ohio: LWF Publications, 1994 (online).

Smith, Robert Barr. "The Cook Gang: Plaguing Indian Territory." *Wild West* (August 2006).

Wellman, Paul I. *A Dynasty of Western Outlaws*. Lincoln: University of Nebraska, 1896.

www.historyoklahoma101.net/cookgang.htm (multiple
contemporary newspaper accounts).

Big-Mouthed Al Jennings

Nix, Evett Dumas. *Oklahombres: Particularly the Wilder Ones.*
Lincoln: University of Nebraska Press, 1993.
Shirley, Glenn. *West of Hell's Fringe: Crime, Criminals, and the Federal
Peace Officer.* Norman: University of Oklahoma Press, 1978.

The Battle of Ingalls

Nix, Evett Dumas. *Oklahombres: Particularly the Wilder Ones.*
Lincoln: University of Nebraska Press, 1993.
Shirley, Glenn. *Gunfight at Ingalls: The Death of an Outlaw Town.*
Stillwater, Okla.: Barbed Wire Press, 1990.
_____. *West of Hell's Fringe: Crime, Criminals, and the Federal
Peace Officer.* Norman: University of Oklahoma Press, 1978.
Smith, Robert Barr. "Shootout at Ingalls." *Wild West* (October 1992).
_____. *Tough Towns: True Tales from the Gritty Streets of the Old
West.* Guilford, Conn.: Globe Pequot Press, 2007.

The Dalton Boys

Dalton, Emmett. *Beyond the Law.* Coffeyville, Kans.: Coffeyville
Historical Society, n.d.
Elliot, David Stewart. *Last Raid of the Daltons and Battle with the
Bandits at Coffeyville, Kansas, Oct. 5, 1892.* Coffeyville, Kans.:
Coffeyville Journal reprint of 1892 book.
Rascoe, Burton. *The Dalton Brothers: By an Eyewitness.* New York:
Frederick Fell, 1954.
Samuelson, Nancy. *The Dalton Gang Story: Lawmen to Outlaws.*

Eastford, Conn.: Shooting Star Press, 1992.

Smith, Robert Barr. *Daltons! The Raid on Coffeyville, Kansas.* Norman: University of Oklahoma Press, 1996.

The Two Faces of Ned Christie

Harmon, S. W. *Hell on the Border: He Hanged Eighty-Eight Men.* Muskogee, Okla.: Indian Heritage Association, 1971.

Shirley, Glenn. *Heck Thomas, Frontier Marshal.* Norman: University of Oklahoma Press, 1981.

Speer, Bonnie Stahlman. *The Killing of Ned Christie.* Norman, Okla.: Reliance Press, 1990.

Steele, Phillip. *The Last Cherokee Warriors.* Gretna, La.: Pelican Publishing Company, 1974.

Henry Starr

Harmon, S. W. *Hell on the Border: He Hanged Eighty-Eight Men.* Muskogee, Okla.: Indian Heritage Association, 1971.

Nix, Evett Dumas. *Oklahombres: Particularly the Wilder Ones.* Lincoln: University of Nebraska Press, 1993.

Shirley, Glenn. *Last of the Real Badmen: Henry Starr.* Lincoln: University of Nebraska Press, 1976.

Curtains for the Verdigris Kid

Smith, Robert Barr. *Tough Town: True Tales from the Gritty Streets of the Old West.* Guilford, Conn.: Globe Pequot Press, 2007.

West, C. W. *Outlaws and Peace Officers of Indian Territory.* Muskogee, Okla.: Muskogee Publishing Company, n.d.

Old Tom Starr

Foreman, Grant. *The Five Civilized Tribes*. Norman: University of Oklahoma Press, 1989.

Shirley, Glenn. *Belle Starr and Her Times*. Norman: University of Oklahoma Press, 1982.

Elmer McCurdy Finds a Job He Can Do

"A Corpse Is a Corpse, Of Course, Unless It's Elmer McCurdy," *Wall Street Journal*, July 11, 1991.

"Bandit Slain in Desperate Fight with Officers," *Daily Oklahoman* (Oklahoma City), September 8, 1911.

Coroner's Report. Los Angeles Medical Examiner-Coroner, No. 76-14812.

Police Department, City of Long Beach, California. Dead Body Report 765 0028.

Snow, Clyde. "The Life and Afterlife of Elmer J. McCurdy: A Melodrama in Two Acts." In *Human Identification: Case Studies in Forensic Anthropology*. Springfield, Ill.: Charles C. Thomas, 1984.

"Train Robber Died to Get into Show Business," *Denver Post*, September 10, 1989.

Belle Starr

Harmon, S. W. *Hell on the Border: He Hanged Eighty-Eight Men*. Muskogee, Okla.: Indian Heritage Association, 1971.

Indian-Pioneer Papers. Interview with Jim McLish. University of Oklahoma Western History Library.

Lavone, Luby. "Desperado: The Infamous Belle Starr." www.geocities.com/laverne/outlaws.

Shirley, Glenn. *Belle Starr and Her Times*. Norman: University of
 Oklahoma Press, 1982.
_____. *West of Hell's Fringe: Crime, Criminals, and the Federal
 Peace Officer*. Norman: University of Oklahoma Press, 1978.
Starr, Myra Maybelle Shirley. *Handbook of Texas Online*. www.tsha.
 utexas.edu/handbook/online.

The Buck Gang

Harmon, S. W. *Hell on the Border: He Hanged Eighty-Eight Men*.
 Muskogee, Okla.: Indian Heritage Association, 1971.
Shirley, Glenn. *Thirteen Days of Terror*. Stillwater, Okla.: Barbed
 Wire Press, 1996.

Al Spencer

Indian-Pioneer Papers. Interview with Ike Nicholson. University of
 Oklahoma Western History Library.
Murray, David. "Al Spencer & Gang."
Oklahombres.org.

The Caseys and the Christians

Burton, Jeff. *Black Jack Christian*. Santa Fe, N.Mex.: Press of the
 Territorian, 1967.
Butler, Ken. *Oklahoma Renegades: Their Deeds and Misdeeds*.
 Gretna, La.: Pelican Publishing Company, 2000.
Shirley, Glenn. *West of Hell's Fringe: Crime, Criminals, and the
 Federal Peace Officer*. Norman: University of Oklahoma Press,
 1978.
Smith, Robert Barr, "Born Bad: The Outlaw Christian Brothers."
 Wild West (December 2000).

Outlaw Heaven

Farris, David A. *Oklahoma Outlaw Tales*. Edmond, Okla.: Little
    Bruce, 1999.
Smith, Robert Barr. "When Outlaws Ruled No Man's Land." *Wild
    West* (February 1999).

The Undistinguished Career of Bill Dalton

Indian-Pioneer Papers. Interview with Mike Gorman. University of
    Oklahoma Western History Library.
"Loot of a Texas Bank," *San Francisco Chronicle*, May 24, 1894.
Nix, Evett Dumas. *Oklahombres: Particularly the Wilder Ones*.
    Lincoln: University of Nebraska Press, 1993.
Preece, Harold. *The Dalton Gang: End of an Outlaw Era*. New
    York: Hastings House, 1963.
Samuelson, Nancy. "Bill Dalton: The Most Mysterious of the
    Dalton Brothers." *Wild West* (June 2004).
_____. *The Dalton Gang Story: Lawmen to Outlaws*. Eastford,
    Conn.: Shooting Star Press, 1992.
Shirley, Glenn. *Six Gun and Silver Star*. Albuquerque: University of
    New Mexico Press, 1955.
_____. *West of Hell's Fringe: Crime, Criminals, and the Federal
    Peace Officer*. Norman: University of Oklahoma Press, 1978.

Bob Rogers

Shirley, Glenn. *Law West of Fort Smith: A History of Frontier Justice
    in the Indian Territory*. Lincoln: University of Nebraska Press,
    1968.

The Martin Boys

_____. *They Outrobbed Them All: The Rise and Fall of the Vicious Martins*. Stillwater, Okla.: Barbed Wire Press, 1992.
When George Birdwell Robbed the Wrong Bank
Smith, Robert Barr. *Tough Towns: True Tales from the Gritty Streets of the Old West*. Guilford, Conn.: Globe Pequot Press, 2007.

The Saga of Zip Wyatt

Cook, Daniel L. *Hands Up!* Norman: University of Oklahoma Press, 1958.
Croy, Homer. *Trigger Marshal The Story of Chris Madsen*. Charleston, S.C.: Nabu Press, 2011.
Nix, Evett Dumas. *Oklahombres: Particularly the Wilder Ones*. Lincoln: University of Nebraska Press, 1993.
Shirley, Glenn. *Six-Gun and Silver Star*. Albuquerque: University of New Mexico Press, 1955.
_____. *West of Hell's Fringe: Crime, Criminals, and the Federal Peace Officer*. Norman: University of Oklahoma Press, 1978.
_____. *Desperado from Cowboy Flat: The Saga of "Zip" Wyatt*. Stillwater, Okla.: Barbed Wire Press, 1998.

Larry DeVol

Edge, L.L. *Run the Cat Roads*. New York: Dembner Books, 1981.
Ernst, Robert R. *Robbin' Banks and Killin' Cops*. Baltimore: Publish America, 2009.
Helmer, William J., and Rick Mattix. *The Complete Public Enemy Almanac*. Nashville, Tenn.: Cumberland House, 2007.
Morgan, R.D. *Taming the Sooner State*. Stillwater, Okla.: New Forums, 2007.
Swierczynski, Duane. *This Here's A Stick-Up*. Indianapolis: Alpha Books, 2002.

Index

Cherokee death cry, 67

Cherokee National Female
 Seminary, 64

Cherokees, 2, 3, 5, 7, 10,
 12, 15, 62, 67, 97, 98,
 101

Cherokee Strip Money, 15

Chitwood Gang, 160

Chouteau, Oklahoma, 18

Christian, Bill, 149, 150,
 151, 152, 153, 154,
 156, 157

Christian, Bob, 149, 150,
 151, 152, 153, 154, 157

Christie, Ned, 61, 62, 64, 65,
 66, 67, 68, 69, 71, 72

Christie, Oklahoma, 4

Christie, Watt, 62, 69, 71

Cimarron, Oklahoma, 191

Citizens' Bank of Lenapah,
 137

Civil War, 2, 3, 101, 114

Claremore, Oklahoma, 18, 27

Clark, Tom, 119

Clemmons, J. R., 176

Clemmons, Tom, 175, 176

Clifton, Dan "Dynamite
 Dick," 27, 30, 36, 38,
 39, 42

Clingan, Lee, 138

Clopton, Ralph, 138, 139

Cochran, Jess, 22, 23

Coe, Bill, 168, 169

Coffeyville Journal, 54, 57

Coffeyville, Kansas, 47, 48,
 55, 56, 57, 60, 76, 81,
 186

Coffman, Cleve, 85, 86, 87

Condon Bank, 48, 50, 51,
 52, 55

Connelly, Charles, 53

Connelly, Slim, 137

Cook, Bill, 10, 13, 14, 15,
 17, 18, 19, 20, 21, 23,
 94

Cook Gang, 10, 12, 15, 16,
 18, 90

Cook, Jim, 10, 12, 13, 14,
 23

Cook, Lou, 10

Copeland, Charlie, 70

Corner, the, 150

Cowboy Flat, Oklahoma,
 209

Craft's Carnival Circus, 109

Crane, Jim, 181

Cravatt, Gus, 191, 192, 197

Creekmore, Milo, 77

Crittenden, Effie, 10

Cross, John, 194, 198

Crosswight, John, 147

Crump, George, 18, 21, 86,
 94, 134

Cumplin, Link, 78

Curry, Paul, 82, 83, 84

Cushing, Oklahoma, 29

D

G

H

Holman, Earl, 142
Homestead Act, 1862, 159
Hopeton, Oklahoma, 193
Houston, Sam, 26
Houston, Sam (ranch hand),
    124, 131
Houston, Sequoyah, 10, 12,
    15
Houston, Temple, 24, 26
Huckleberry, James, 6
Hueston, Tom, 37, 38, 43
Hull family, 189
Humphrey, Dick, 72
Hutchinson, Kansas, 223

I

Independent Order of Odd
    Fellows, 194
Indian Home Guard, 2
Indian Journal, 91, 94
Indian Territory Posse of
    Westerners, 113
Ingalls, Oklahoma, 35, 172
Ingalls, Oklahoma, fight, 35
Iron Mountain Railway, 89
Irwin, Sam, 22, 23
Isbel, L. P., 65, 66
Isham's Hardware, 50, 52,
    53

J

Jackson, Jesse, 76
James brothers, the, 102
James, Frank, 48
James, Jesse, 48, 81
James-Younger Gang, 13,
    175
Jared, Walter, 105
Jennings, Al, 24, 26, 27, 29,
    31, 32, 33, 34, 150
Jennings, Ed, 24, 26
Jennings, Frank, 27, 31, 32
Jennings, John, 24, 26
Johnson, Crook-Neck, 156
Johnson, Jess, 154
Johnson, J. J., 87
Johnson, Julia, 45, 58
Jones, Arkansas Tom, 35,
    38, 39, 40, 173, 182
Jones, Jim, 175
Jones, Milt, 152, 153
Jones, Will, 175
July, Maoma, 122, 126, 130

K

Kansas City Massacre, 225
Kansas City Times, 18
Karpis, Alvin, 223, 224, 225
Keating, Francis, 223, 225
Keetoowahs, 3, 4, 7, 71
Kelly, Curtis, 143, 145

About the Author

Robert Barr Smith is a law professor at the University of Oklahoma and a retired colonel, US Army. He is the author of eleven books and almost 150 articles on western and military history. A senior parachutist, he served in Vietnam, Germany, and all across the United States. He is a frequent lecturer on the West.